A FISH IN ALIEN STREAMS

Herjinder Singh Sahni is a writer and senior journalist. Starting as a sub-editor with *Navbharat Times*, he has worked with renowned media houses over the last three decades, including the Times of India Group, India Today Group and Hindustan Times Group, as well as various magazines, television channels and online portals. On his YouTube channel 'अतीत The Past by Herjinder', he talks about little-known nuggets of Indian and world history. When not writing or working, Herjinder can be found travelling in the lap of nature or discussing food and history with his friends and family.

A FISH IN ALIEN STREAMS

The Incredible Journey of the Trout in India

HERJINDER

FOREWORD BY RAMACHANDRA GUHA

hachette INDIA

First published in 2021 by Hachette India
(Registered name: Hachette Book Publishing India Pvt. Ltd)
An Hachette UK company
www.hachetteindia.com

SRD

ISBN 978-93-91028-70-1

Hachette Book Publishing India Pvt. Ltd
4th & 5th Floors, Corporate Centre
Plot No. 94, Sector 44, Gurugram – 122003, India

Typeset in Mrs Eaves 12.5/15.3
by Manmohan Kumar, Delhi

Printed and bound in India
by Manipal Technologies Limited, Manipal

FSC www.fsc.org
MIX
Paper from responsible sources
FSC™ C104740

CONTENTS

FOREWORD

RAMACHANDRA GUHA

EARLY IN 2020, I GOT A CALL FROM THE AUTHOR OF THIS book. We had known each other for more than a decade, in which time I had come to admire him for the depth of his political understanding and for his bilingual skills. He was one of the journalists in the Indian media I most respected. Based on our earlier exchanges, I presumed he had called to speak about some matter of contemporary import. I was mistaken. He wished to talk to me about a manuscript he had written on a very different subject altogether. He asked whether he could send me a draft. I had, in the past, inflicted on him many things I had written, so, as much out of guilt as of interest, I said yes.

A few days later, a soft copy of this history of trout fishing in India arrived in my inbox. I began reading it, at first with curiosity, but increasingly with fascination. Here was a remarkable and long-forgotten tale, told with care, understanding, empathy, and, not least, authority.

I knew that it was out of homesickness that the British in India began playing sports such as cricket and football amongst themselves, in time encouraging – or perhaps provoking – their subjects to play these games too. I now discovered that it was out of even more intense feelings of homesickness that the British had brought their favourite species of fish to these alien shores.

However, building cricket pitches and starting white-only clubs in India were child's play compared to acclimatizing trout in India. Back in the nineteenth century, well before air travel had been invented, to successfully bring live trout across the oceans constituted an enormous challenge. So that at least some individuals survived, one had to transport a decent number of fish, keeping them going with fresh flowing water abundant in oxygen during the weeks and months the ship spent on the seas. The effort – in time, money, intellectual focus and organizational energy – was colossal, almost comparable to fighting a war even.

There were, as this book so vividly describes, many initial failures, but these madly obsessive Englishmen would not be deterred. Local Indian fish did not remotely pose the sort of challenge to anglers that their beloved trout did. Finally, an intrepid entrepreneur succeeded in successfully domesticating this exotic species in the rivers of Kashmir, from where it spread to other parts of the subcontinent.

Given the author's background, this book, appropriately, began as a news story. In 2009 he travelled to the hills of Himachal Pradesh to write about the hundredth anniversary of the introduction of trout in the state. As he candidly confesses, when he set out for the assignment 'my knowledge of fish of any kind was limited'. He wrote the article, its word length compelling him to leave out much of the material he had collected. But the subject stayed with him, and we must be grateful that it did, as the much more extensive research he since did has resulted in this wonderful book.

A Fish in Alien Streams is wonderfully wide-ranging in space and time, and in its cast of characters. Beginning in the first half of the nineteenth century, the narrative extends right into the present. This is a tricontinental story, about Europe and Asia of course, but also, quite crucially, about Oceania, since trout was successfully acclimatized in Tasmania well before India, and since some colonial officials from Australia sought energetically to replicate their success in the largest colony of the Empire.

Within India, the narrative of *A Fish in Alien Streams* extends from Kashmir and Kullu in the north to the Nilgiris and Travancore in the south, taking in Ceylon as well. The book is peopled with a range of eccentric and engaging individuals, whose stories are sensitively told. The hill and river landscapes are vividly evoked. The obsessions of the fishermen are captured with unerring accuracy and rich detail.

A Fish in Alien Streams is based on an enormous amount of primary research, conducted in archives and libraries across India. The author draws upon many rare books and journal articles written by soldiers, travellers, missionaries, scientists and colonial administrators. He digs deeply into the scientific literature on fishes and fish species. Yet, this learning is carried lightly and conveyed with clarity. Among the joys of the book are the vivid quotations from letters, documents, memoirs and travelogues.

It has been a privilege all these years to have known Herjinder as a professional colleague, and a pleasure now to be asked to write a foreword to *A Fish in Alien Streams*. This book is a noteworthy contribution to natural history as well as to social history. I strongly recommend it to nature lovers, and all those interested in the curious and controversial career of British colonialism in India.

PROLOGUE

IT WAS A CHILLY MORNING IN JANUARY 2009 WHEN I arrived in Patlikuhal, a small hill village on the banks of the Beas River off National Highway 3. This sleepy village in Himachal Pradesh is barely a dot on the tourism map, but where this village ends, the popular town of Manali begins. From here too the road bifurcates, one branch leading to Naggar, a small but very beautiful town which was once the capital of the hill state of Kullu. Naggar Castle and the house of the legendary Russian artist Nicholas Roerich are prime attractions here for thousands of tourists.

Every few years, though, Patlikuhal makes news: when there is heavy snowfall and the highway is blocked. Apart from being an important junction for trips to Manali and Naggar, the village also has a school that teaches Tibetan fine art. And, of late, Patlikuhal has gained another reason for modest renown – its state government-owned rainbow trout farm, established along a roaring hilly stream.

This trout farm was where I was headed when I arrived in 2009. It was the centenary year of the introduction of trout in Himachal Pradesh, when trout eggs were brought to the Kullu Valley and the fish were reared successfully. I had been commissioned to write an article on this historic event for the Hindi magazine *Kadambini*, published by the Hindustan Times Group.

I was not unacquainted with this aquatic beauty. Travelling to Manali from Himachal's Mandi district and crossing the Aut Tunnel, it is impossible to miss signboards announcing the presence of trout in the area. Several restaurants here invite the visitor to partake of delicacies such as tandoori trout, masala trout, butter trout and the like. So I had already encountered trout, but only at these restaurants.

Like any reasonably conscientious journalist, I did a little homework on the internet and read up a bit about Himachal Fisheries. I thought the assignment was simple enough: take a look at the fisheries' infrastructure in the Kullu–Manali area, write in some history and then submit my article. I planned to stay a week hoping that, in addition to writing about trout, I would be able to make the time count for half a dozen other feature articles. And, of course, I was pleased that this assignment would take me to one of India's most beautiful valleys.

At the trout farm in Patlikuhal, I saw for the first time a number of healthy trout of different ages and sizes, swimming in artificial canals built for the purpose. Farm officials described in detail the methods of raising them. Later that day, I was taken to the rainbow trout hatchery nearby, also owned by the government of Himachal

Pradesh. There, too, the entire process of taking care of the ova and nurturing them to grow into tiny fish in a few weeks was detailed to me. When they become fingerlings they are moved to the trout farm, I was told. I also visited several trout farms run by the private sector. And, of course, met the trout on my plate at dinner.

The next day I was to meet some old-time residents of Kullu. Within a few hours and after only a couple of meetings, it became clear to me that all that I had read and seen about trout was of no use for my story. Trying to understand the brown trout brought to the Kullu Valley a hundred years ago in a rainbow trout farm was akin to trying to understand the history of the wild chicken in a poultry farm.

Among the people I met was S.B. Raizada, a Kullu environmentalist who was once a fisheries officer in the Himachal Pradesh government. He retired to live in Seobagh, a village on the left bank of the Beas. A short meeting at his house changed the direction of my story. Or, perhaps more accurately, gave my story the right orientation. This is not unusual in journalism, where every orientation presupposes a few disorientations.

The first thing I understood was that, while I had come to research a story on trout in Kullu, this was not in fact the first port of arrival for trout fish from Europe. Its passage to India had started much earlier.

At the same time, it was also evident that my story could not merely be about the immigrant fish that had made Indian rivers their home. It must also be about the passion of a few expatriates who were unable to settle comfortably in India without their favourite fish and their favourite pastime.

My work now became more difficult. All the homework had to be done anew. When I tried to research the subject, I found only limited information online. I would have to dig deep into physical archives and libraries too. I was a fish-eater myself but I had been raised in a non-fish-eating community of north India, and my knowledge of fish of any kind was limited. But the journey taught me a lot about the fish whose history I was seeking, as well as about the river systems of India and how they have changed over the course of a century.

I completed and submitted my article on time. After it was published, it even won some praise. But I felt a sense of dissatisfaction – there was a lot the story had had to leave out because of space constraints and insufficient research. That was when I decided to write a book, hoping that it might be able to do justice to the subject in a way that a four-page magazine article could not.

I had no idea at the time that it would take me more than a decade to collect the material to write the book. I had a full-time newspaper job, and had to do my research at the National Archives in Delhi after taking leave or in my spare time. I travelled to the Punjab State Archives in Chandigarh as well as the Himachal State Archives in Shimla. My quest for old and out-of-print books led me to the National Library in Kolkata, from where I returned with plenty of information and some wonderful experiences. I had bought many books and had got the chance to peruse the personal collections of several people. The website www.archive.org was an excellent resource too.

Finally, after more than a decade of work, I have been able to write a book on a subject I knew virtually nothing about when I found myself in Patlikuhal on a cold winter's day in 2009.

I
NO TRUE TROUT IN INDIA

IT WAS THE HOTTEST DAY OF THE HOTTEST MONTH OF the year. Henry Stedman Polehampton, chaplain of Lucknow, capital of the north Indian state of Oudh, was feeling homesick. On 17 June 1856, he wrote a letter to his brother in England, which ran:

> MY DEAR EDWARD,
>
> Pray do send me a diary. Every scrap from England is interesting, and your letters are feasted on as they arrive. I thank you for your fresh assurances of affection to me…
>
> I had in my mind's eye at the moment our paddling up that brook at Pontesbury together last summer. What a pleasant day that was, and what a nice lot of trout we killed!

Four months later, suffering from a high fever, the Chaplain wrote a letter to his mother: 'I do so long to spend some of my last days among the sweet solitude of the "Walls" and of the lovely little valley, where the trout-brook runs...'

Polehampton was not alone in these sentiments. In the nineteenth and twentieth centuries, very many Europeans in India were pining for the salmon and the trout, superior game-fish of their native lands. Most of these Europeans were British, employees of the East India Company and its army. Some were Christian missionaries who had come to perform the divine duty of proselytizing the masses. Some were French and German experts working for the armed forces of Maharaja Ranjit Singh of Punjab and other princely states, some in the name of modernizing their military strategy, others for making gunpowder, and a few for brewing fine wine for Indian royalty. Then there was an assortment of travellers, adventure-seekers, occasional visitors, and a few settlers. But civil and military servants of the imperial state made up the overwhelming majority.

The British first came to the sub-continent as traders. In their quest for commerce, they created an empire. They were here to stay, and they tried their best to refashion their new environment, attempting to create a rough replica of their homeland that would be at a remove from the local culture. They had almost everything they could want by way of recreation. They could enjoy horse riding, they could play golf, cricket, and other outdoor or indoor games. They could hunt in the dense forests – shoot ibex, bear, bison, barasingha, even tigers and lions. They could go angling in the hilly streams, mighty rivers and magnificent lakes of this sprawling sub-continent.

Upland destinations at a number of beautiful spots in the hills were developed by the British for cool holidays. Initially, these hill stations were intended as temporary escapes from the heat and disease of the plains. But they provided the British with not only seasonal relief from a harsh climate but also from the psychological pressures of an alien culture. The hill stations were developed on a British pattern – with footpaths, trees, flowers, fruit orchards and vegetable gardens, everything was reminiscent of their native land. Soon they decided to established military cantonments and political headquarters at these places too. Apart from their administrative importance, hill stations acted as recreational spaces for the British, offering endless opportunities for sports, parties and gossip.

Despite all these diversions, the hill stations still suffered from a serious lack: no salmon or trout were to be found in these parts. The colonial adventurers had grown up on stories about salmon and trout, savouring paintings of these beautiful fish, and relishing eating them. Now, in an alien land, they searched everywhere for salmon and trout, in mountain creeks, in meadow streams, in small ponds, in big lakes and in large rivers. Even a rumour of the sighting of a trout-like fish was enough to make someone rush off to confirm or deny it.

In the early 1830s, when John McClelland heard about 'a species of trout which differs from any variety known in Great Britain' in the hills of Kumaon, he immediately packed his knapsack to find out for himself. McClelland was a medical doctor by profession, but a geologist and biologist by inclination. On his expedition, he found a fish that was locally known as *gulabi machhli* (pink fish) which, unfortunately, had 'no affinity to trout'. Later, he wrote in the *Journal of the Asiatic Society of Bengal* in 1835 that, 'from the appearance of this species it has commonly been considered by Europeans to whom it is familiar as a common mountain trout; a closer examination, however, soon detects the mistake, and except that it belongs to the class of abdominal fishes and inhabit fresh water streams, there is no natural connexion between this fish and the species to which it was supposed to belong.' It was, in fact, *Barilius bola*, which is a carp. Soon, McClelland found that it was not even a good sport fish; nonetheless, as a naturalist, he studied it in detail.

Then there was the 'Himalayan trout', a fish in Kashmir locally known as *chiru*, which proved to be no trout but a temperate *Schizothorax*. Another fish that received attention was one known as the 'snow trout', but which was actually a glacial zone *Schizothoraichthys*. Though these local fish had the appearance and many habits of trout, the fish of the *Salmonidae* subfamily, which held a special place in the heart of Europeans, were nowhere to be found in India. As the *Imperial Gazetteer of India* baldly, and somewhat gloomily, stated in its first volume, 'No Salmonidae are known in India or Burma; the nearest locality where any Salmonid occurs is north of Afghanistan in the upper tributaries of the Oxus.' The *Gazetteer* declared that there were 'no true trout in India'.

Some of those who tried to search for these fish, such as Lt. Col. S.J. Thomson of the Indian Medical Service, wrote more eloquently of this dispiriting fact. In his book, *The Silent India: Being Tales and Sketches of the Masses* published in 1913, he wrote: 'There are also hill-trout which take the fly, to be caught in the smaller streams, but they are very poor imitations of our English fish.'

In his book *Cyclopaedia of India and of Eastern and Southern Asia* published in 1835, Surgeon-General Edward Balfour, who was a corresponding member of the Imperial-Royal Geological Institute, Vienna, as well as a fellow of Madras University, remarked:

> Hill trout of Hindustan is no trout, but a large bony fish of a silver-grey spotted with black; will eat everything he can swallow; is often taken with an infant brother while spinning for his high-caste neighbours, with an artificial minnow of glass, with a piece of rag or newspaper, with bees, or dragon-flies caught off the bushes by the river, with a morsel of cabbage leaves boiled, but in general with the orthodox-spinning, the minnow, or the artificial fly, made very large and showy. In Kashmir, five bags of these fish have been caught, some weighing 7 lbs. each. One seen in the market was 19 lbs. The Walur Lake, the Dhul Lake, and the Jhelum all swarm with them about the mulberry trees, the fallen fruits of which

> seem to afford them in legions a sweet and pleasant diet, if one may judge by the mighty rush ensuing on a shaking of the boughs. ...This fish is widely distributed; abundant in the backwaters of the Ganges, in the great rapids of that river far above Hurdwar, and in Dehra Doon, in lat. 27° 28 N., in the upper branches of the Brahmaputra, and in the Mishmi and Abor backwaters, also in most of the small rivers of the Panjab, in which latter locality it does not seem to grow very large, though plentifully, owing perhaps to its being the common food of numerous fish of prey. Is abundant, though small, in Central India, in Bundelkhand and Jhansi districts. That it is eatable, is all that can be said, but giving good sport in its way, and yielding subsistence to the monsters of the deep, and useful in diverting their attention from mischief to their own breed.

The fiction of the time also reflected the fact of this keenly felt absence. Thomas Capt. Mayne Reid, an Irish-American novelist, wrote a novel in 1858 titled *The Plant Hunters; or, Adventures Among the Himalaya Mountains*. One of its characters says, 'I think there are fish in the lake. I have heard there is a very eatable kind of fish in all rivers of the Himalayas, known as "Himalayan trout"– though it is misnamed, for it is not a trout but a species of carp. I am sure I have seen trout leap in the lake. Let us try a fly to-day.'

The most interesting piece of fiction about trout in India was published in *Bentley's Miscellany*, a literary magazine edited by Charles Dickens. In Volume XLI, published in 1857, three letters bore the title 'A Fisherman's Letter to his Chum in India'. These are letters from an English fisherman to his friend Harry, who was working in India. In the first letter the fisherman wrote about some of his trout fishing adventures:

> I fancy I see you stretched on your sofa, with a nargileh in your mouth and your "Salmonia" opened in your hand, almost weeping; not like the great Alexander because there were no more worlds to win, but there are no trout and salmon to slay in the tropics. I confess I very often pity you; but, why did you enlist?...
>
> I have kept my promise, and send you a description of two spirited encounters. I find many other notes, but have no time at present to write more to you. So adieu!
>
> When you have digested my letter (which, I fear, has tantalized as much as it has pleased you), go to your dinner "with what appetite you may", and don't throw the dish of curry at poor Sambo's head because he has not brought you a salmon cutlet...!

There are no historical records of how many dishes of curry were thrown at native servants because they didn't bring their sahibs salmon cutlets. However, by this time, most Europeans colonists had realized that life without trout and salmon was a hard fact of existence in India.

There were nonetheless some Englishmen who managed to enjoy angling in the sub-continent despite the lack of trout and salmon. In his book *Angling in the Kumaun Lakes* published in 1888, W. Walker wrote:

> Europeans have scarcely yet begun to realize that, while sweltering in the Courts of Agra, Allahabad or Benares, soul and body at the point of giving way to the depressing influences of work and climate, they are actually within a few hours' journey of splendid sport in a charming climate, amidst some of the loveliest scenery in the world, to which they can flee away from the dust and the heat and the weary monotony of hot-weather life in the plains...

These pleasure-seeking colonists were trying to find substitutes for trout in indigenous Indian fish. At a number of places, they even formed angling associations and clubs to promote their shared interest. Notable among these were the Nilgiri Fishing Association, the Dehradun Fishing Association, the Central Province Fishing Association in Jabalpur, the Myitkyina Fishing Club (north Burma), the North Punjab Fishing Club, the Palani Hills Game Association in Kodaikanal, the High Range Angling Association in Munnar and the Angling Association in Tezpur, Assam. The main activity of these organisations was to share information about local rivers, streams, lakes, available varieties of fishes and fishing equipment. G.H. Lacy, Honorary Secretary of the North Punjab Fishing Association, even compiled an *Angler's Handbook*, published by W. Newman & Company, in 1888.

The nineteenth-century American traveller William Taylor Adams (who wrote books under the pseudonym 'Oliver Optic'), in his 1895 book *Across India: Or, Live Boys in the Far East*, recalled an event in Bombay where the European guests…

> …went to the saloon in which dinner was served, closely followed by their servants; and the scene there was decidedly unique to the Americans, for there were as many servants as guests. The hotel furnishes no attendants, and each visitor brings his own. But as soon as all were seated, order came out of confusion and the service proceeded. The dishes were somewhat peculiar; but Sir Modava explained them to the commander.… "I think you will find this fish very good," said his lordship, as the second course came on, "It is the bummaloti, sometimes called the Bombay duck, something like both the salmon and the trout. It is a salt-water fish, abundant off this coast, where it is extensively taken, salted, and dried, to be sent to all parts of India."

Henry Sullivan Thomas of the Madras Civil Service found the legendary Indian fish, the mahseer, similarly appealing. 'Having caught him, then to eat him,' he wrote, 'you and your friends will find he is well flavoured, and very rich, so rich that you will want no melted butter or other sauce with him, and so rich that you will not be able to eat over-much of him. To my thinking he is the best eating fish in Indian fresh waters, and stands between the salmon and the trout for the table.'

Thomas's book, *The Rod in India* published in 1873, is in fact a guide to catch the mahseer. He writes:

> From this point of view it is that I say a Mahseer shows more sport than a salmon. Not that you can kill more of them, which you may also do, but that each individual Mahseer makes a better fight than a salmon of the same size. I am prepared to expect that on this point, as on most others not capable of being proved to demonstration, some will disagree with me. ...For my own part I can only say that my prejudices were all in favour of the salmon, both as being a salmon, a sort of lion of the waters, whom I had grown up looking on with respect from my childhood, and as being a fellow-countryman. But the Mahseer compelled me to believe in and honour him in spite of my prejudgment to the contrary.

Thomas's book became so popular that, after reading it, the famous angler Maj. J.L. Dickie decided to make a trip to India just for the mahseer. In his book, *Forty Years of Trout and Salmon Fishing* published in 1919, Dickie wrote about visiting India in 1895. About the mahseer, Dickie remarked:

> I have only fished some of the smaller rivers for Mahseer, and have never killed anything very large, so that I cannot claim in any way to be an authority on the subject, but any man who can kill salmon can kill mahseer. The

> largest fish are very seldom got on fly, but usually on spoon, and it is worthwhile to take a good selection of spoons with one to the East, as they do not perish like other tackle. ...It has always been a matter of regret to me that I never was able to go up the Brahmaputra to Suddya, where Mahseer are very plentiful, and where some very big ones are to be had.

Several British anglers, such as Surgeon-General Balfour, were in agreement with Thomas. In his book, Balfour, who was also a well-known orientalist and pioneering environmentalist, and head of the Madras Medical Department, wrote:

> The Indian mahsir are only to be caught from dawn to eleven, or from late in the afternoon till dusk. Its favourite haunts are in the rocky fastnesses of rapid rivers flowing from the hills. Mahsir run not unfrequently to 40 lbs., and even 50 lbs., and show more sport than a salmon. When the rod is stiff, the first pull on the tackle is great. Unlike the salmon and the trout, the mahsir, except under peculiar circumstances, is only to be taken in clear water; and in clear water, under cloudless skies, the angler must make himself and his tackle as little conspicuous as possible. Like all fish that inhabit rough water, it is, of course, extremely vigorous; and, as it runs out the line over a rocky bottom, the angler is very likely to be 'broken'. The mahsir does not hold out so long as the salmon, but the fight while it lasts is more

exciting, the first struggles being more violent, and the rush more impetuous.

Unlike Thomas, Lt. Col. Cecil Lang was not prejudiced in favour of either salmon or trout. Lang wrote a book in 1906, primarily on the mahseer, titled *The Angler in India: Or The Mighty Mahseer*. There are a number of editions of this book available. Some editions have the author's name as Cecil Lang, whereas in others the writer is called Skene Dhu, which was in fact Lang's pen name. The focus of Thomas's book was primarily the rivers, streams and water bodies of south India, whereas Lang wrote mostly about north India.

Lang praised the mahseer thus:

> As a fisherman and an Englishman, however, one is always thought to believe, that given yourself at the one end of the rod and a salmon at the other, the summit of human bliss is reached. And this being in India, substitute mahseer for salmon, and there you are, still at the summit of human bliss. It is I know a much disputed subject, given weight for weight, which is the finer fish. But comparisons are odious, and as 6,000 odd miles divide them, there is no need of rivalry to exist at all.'

Yet many British anglers in India remained nostalgic for trout and mourned its absence in the waters they fished in. An interesting account of this nostalgia was given by Charles Raikes, commissioner of Lahore, in his book *The Englishman in India* published in 1867. Raikes wrote:

> We allow the physical privation and suffering of cutcherry work in the hot season, to be served; but when the sun gives some respite, there are many enjoyments in store for the man of simple tastes and contented mind. Then is the time to sally out into the field amongst the people. Amidst their villages, under the shade of tent or mango grove, the wanderer may almost forget that he is in a strange land. India need not, and can not rival England in our affections. We miss the hills and dales, the steaming pasture, the clear trout streams of our native land; still we may rejoice in the rural beauties of less-favoured scene. The freshness of an Indian morning in the cold season may charm us, if only by contrast.

Many anglers were unable to shake off memories of salmon or trout while spending their day seeking mahseer on the bank of a stream in India. The first sentence of G.H. Lacy's book runs: 'Fishing in India, when generally spoken about, usually refers to the Mahseer, and therefore, unless otherwise stated, all the following notes are intended to apply to Mahseer fishing, which fish takes the lead in India in the same manneras – only in even a greater proportion – than the Salmon does in Great Britain.'

Edward Percy Stebbing, pioneering British forester and entomologist, commended a stream in the Chittagong Hill Tracts (now in Bangladesh) for offering the angler good mahseer fishing in his 1920 book *The Diary of a Sportsman Naturalist in India*.

And in an essay published in *The Sportsman's Book for India* in 1904, the Bengal civil servant Sir Edward Charles Buck wrote:

> The mahseer (big-head) is a carp which imitates the habits and ways of a salmon. Coming up from the giant rivers instead of the sea to spawn in the mountain streams, it affords in the latter excellent sport in spring and autumn[...] Mahseer will be found in exactly the same sort of runs or pools in which you would look for a salmon or a trout. Beginners can only learn this by experience. As you will fish for the most part in very clear water, common sense will be sufficient to teach you that great care in the matter of concealment is necessary... Play your fish as you would a salmon, avoid sudden checks, keep the line always taut but be always ready to yield to a rush, better not try to use a gaff, a net is useful, but big fish should be lifted out of the water by an attendant.

One way to redress such quantities of aching nostalgia for their favourite fish was, of course, to bring the freshwater beauty from Britain to India. But, in the late nineteenth century, this was deemed almost impossible. Today trout is the most widely spread cold water species of fish, present in almost all continents, but at that time the only country where it had transmigrated was Russia, which was neither very far nor very different from Western Europe.

Trout is a true coldwater fish; it can survive only in temperatures well under 14°C. A number of mountainous locations in India met this condition but the problem was a tremendous one of logistics. How did one transport, across a distance of 5,000 miles, live fish that needed a constant supply of fresh, flowing, cold water with plenty of oxygen? Commercial aviation started only in 1914; in India it started 18 years later in 1932, and only for short distances, such as between Karachi and Bombay. In the nineteenth century, the only link between India and Europe was the sea route, and commercial ships took a full 40 days to make this journey. Neither the fish nor its eggs could survive such a long passage; the eggs hatch in two weeks into tiny creatures called alevin or sac fry, which are ready to swim into fresh, flowing water.

The problems were considerable, but were they insurmountable?

II

SUCCESS IN TASMANIA

THE LONGING FOR TROUT AMONG EUROPEANS IN GENERAL, and the British in particular, was not a phenomenon specific to India. In faraway Australia, this sentiment was just as strong among homesick colonials, especially in the British crown colony of Tasmania. These settlers of the hilly Australian island with cold weather had little interest in local fish. Fishing clubs and anglers' associations in Tasmania were hubs of ill-suppressed longing, all members waiting for the day when they would be able to fish for trout. The island's 3,000-odd lakes and numerous cold rivers and streams would have all been congenial homes for salmon and trout but there was no such fishing to be had. The desire to introduce Atlantic salmon and brown trout into Tasmania's – and Victoria and New South Wales' – plentiful water bodies became stronger and stronger.

The first attempts to introduce trout to Tasmania date to when that island was still known as Van Diemen's Land. In 1841, a certain Captain Frederick Chalmers had an outrageous idea: of importing salmon and trout ova from Europe. He wrote to a fish breeder in Scotland, his plan being that the fish eggs could be placed in a basket filled with gravel and then put in a bucket of water to be transported on the deck of a ship. This plan indicated that Captain Chalmers had little idea about the practicalities of trout and salmon breeding. As other such enquiries began to arrive in the fisheries of Europe, it was made clear that such methods could succeed only if the water was cold enough and if the entire process of transportation was completed in under a month. However, this was a time before the Suez Canal was built, when ships had to take a much longer route, rounding the southern coast of Africa via the Cape of Good Hope. The journey from England to Australia took more than three months.

A few years after Captain Chalmers's original enquiry, the lieutenant governor of Tasmania, Sir William Thomas Denison, revived the proposal. His own favourite pastimes were riding, angling and shooting. He wanted to introduce both salmon and trout in the Great Lake of the island, hoping to make the place an angling resort. The task was assigned to Gottlieb Boccius, a well-known fish-keeper and writer. On 3 February 1852, Boccius left a British port in a vessel called the *Columbus*, taking with him 50,000 ova (in the form of spawn) of salmon and trout. He stored them in a wooden tank that contained 60 gallons of water, and decided to pour in six gallons of fresh water every four hours. He expected that both the salmon and trout would hatch around mid April but, in March, when he was off the African coast, he could see small fry swimming in the tub. Van Diemen's Land was still very far away and soon, when the water began to warm, it would be impossible for the little fish to survive. Along with the time and effort, the 300 pounds spent on the project went to waste.

Gottlieb Boccius prepared a detailed report on this failed venture, as published in the second volume of *Papers and Proceedings of the Royal Society of Van Damien's Land* in 1852, and steeled himself for another such experiment. He wrote, with some confidence:

> Had this delay not occurred combined with the unfortunate detention, as Captain Smith states in his report – the weather throughout being intensely hot, with a vertical sun for many days – that was from 1st to 14th March, I have not the slightest doubt that the first experiment would have been perfectly successful: and although it proved a failure, the experiment produced the positive fact, that the salmon and trout are bred out on a shipboard and at sea, which hitherto has never been achieved, [and] negative all the theories of every former authority upon the habit of the salmonidae. I am therefore quite certain of the success of a second undertaking.

The Lieutenant Governor of Tasmania was also very keen to take another shot at the experiment, and permission and funds for a second attempt were issued immediately. But this attempt did not succeed either. This time a cruel British winter took its toll and the entire batch of harvesting spawn was frozen out to lifelessness.

These two failures notwithstanding, some years later, votaries of importing salmon and trout into Australia became active again. Among them, Edward Wilson, editor of the Melbourne newspaper *The Argus*, was especially vocal. He even founded the Acclimatisation Society of Victoria, for salmon. On a visit to London, Wilson met James Arndell Youl, a Tasmanian educated in England and on the prowl for adventure. Wilson tasked Youl with the job, and offered him 600 pounds by way of reward. Unlike Gottlieb Boccius, Youl did not have a background in, or any particular understanding of, fish breeding, but his resolve was much stronger. Studying the matter carefully, he identified the two biggest challenges as being packaging and transport.

Youl first managed a trial shipment of salmon eggs in 1860. He booked 15 tonnes worth of ice space on an American clipper named *Sarah Carling*. On this expanse of ice, he built two rooms, one within the other. Trays were placed there at a slight angle, so that cold water could flow continuously. Meanwhile, Youl was joined by Robert Ramsbottom, a reputable salmon breeder, who collected 30,000 salmon ova from the Dovey river in Wales. The ship sailed from Liverpool, on 25 February 1860, with an attendant on board to remove dead eggs from the lot. But within 59 days the entire lot was dead, due to fungal decay. The only consolation this experiment offered was that the eggs had, for the first time, got as far as the southern hemisphere. This was enough to satisfy the Tasmanian government, which agreed to fund yet another effort, this time with more ice.

The ice was increased to 25 tonnes, and a small steamer named *Beautiful Star* was hired. Ramsbottom's son William accompanied the cargo with 80,000 eggs, again taken from the Dovey river. But the ship ran into a storm and was forced to retreat to Sicily for repairs. The ova began to hatch and, with only a small quantity of ice left, it became more and more difficult to keep them alive. Soon there were no live eggs left at all.

With this failure, tempers began to run high. Youl was castigated for wasting public money by both the local press and by the Salmon Commission appointed by the Tasmanian government. Undaunted, Youl decided to continue his attempt to pack the fish eggs perfectly for a long journey, this time with private funds.

Meanwhile, some fishing experts had begun to discuss the possibility of 'retard hatching' of the ova. They believed that with ice-cold water, the hatching could be delayed by a few weeks. Youl now wanted to apply the process of retard hatching in the packaging itself. His experiment with fish ova in the ice house at London's Crystal Palace, using ice from the Wenham Ice Company, was already in motion. Youl spent almost ten years trying to find the perfect mix for packing. He even travelled across Western Europe to learn more. In France, he discovered that breeders used live moss to pack eyed ova (the stage of egg development when trout ova can be seen with two black dots, i.e., eyes of the future fish).

Youl then started experimenting with pine boxes and moss. Boxes sized 12x8x5 inches were built such that they could hold ice on top. These small boxes of pine wood were perforated from all sides, to allow iced water to pass through. A layer of charcoal was placed in the box to absorb the carbonic gas produced by the odd dying ova. With this packing mix, Youl was able to keep ova alive for more than 140 days – without light, air, or a continuous water supply. Youl seemed to have finally hit upon a winning formula for the transportation of ova.

When the news of this successful experiment reached Tasmania, the government was persuaded to allow one more shipment. This time, Youl was confident of success. William Ramsbottom had also arrived in London to assist him. First, they began to search for a ship that could sail more swiftly to Australia. Youl was lucky enough to be offered 50 tonnes of ice space in the super-fast clipper *Norfolk*, free of charge. The *Norfolk* would be ready to sail from England by 20 January 1864.

Meanwhile, a fresh problem was brewing. While the other arrangements were in place, Youl did not find any fish eggs in the Ribble, nor in the Dovey, nor even the Tyne. A desperate Youl then issued a public appeal to salmon breeders in the United Kingdom, as noted by Charles Rangeley-Wilson in *Silt Road: The Story of a Lost River* published in 2013. He pleaded in *The Times*: 'I may now lose the only chance I ever had of fairly trying to get this noble fish out to Australia.'

Barely two days before the *Norfolk* was to sail, ova started to arrive in London – from Scotland and Lancashire, from Wales and Worcestershire. Some 3,000 brown trout ova were sent by Admiral Henry Keppel, a highly decorated Royal Navy officer and a fish-breeding enthusiast. Keppel had also contacted two famous naturalists, Frank Buckland and Francis Francis. A well-known breeder and writer, Buckland had been following the pine box experiment closely. He collected eggs from the Itchen river while Francis sourced them from the Wey.

Youl and Ramsbottom worked round the clock to pack the 100,000 eggs that had been sent to them. They were packed in 181 boxes and placed on the floor of the ice house of the ship and the Wenham Lake ice was piled on top of this. These boxes were then shipped to Edward Wilson in Melbourne, Youl's friend in the Australian Association and president of the Acclimatisation Society of Victoria. The *Norfolk* reached the Railway Pier, Melbourne, on 15 April 1864, some three months after departing from London.

When Wilson and Ramsbottom opened the door of the ice room, they found that more than three-quarters of the eggs had survived. Youl's plan had worked. An overjoyed Wilson wrote to Youl in London, as published in *Silt Road*:

> The salmon is safe and your statue is secure, it will be erected over the future fish market in Hobart Town,

and you are to be in the attitude of the Medicean Venus, with salmon instead of dolphin. My eyes are failing me but my heart is still in place; and even with one foot in the grave and the other in a pan of salmon ova, I say three cheers for Youl and the *Norfolk*...

The fish eggs, though they had crossed the seven seas, were still far from their final destination. These boxes, containing the eggs and with the ice in them, were then shifted to a ship named the *Victoria*, which was bound for Hobart, across the Bass Strait. From Hobart they were further towed by two row boats to a jetty near the Ark Inn. They were then taken over four miles of very rough country, to a hatchery on the bank of the River Plenty, which was prepared in advance and waiting impatiently for its precious consignment. Ramsbottom unpacked the boxes there and found about 30,000 salmon and 300 trout ova had survived. They were placed in hatching boxes.

On 4 May 1864, brown trout was successfully hatched in the Southern Hemisphere. The very next day an Atlantic salmon arrived. Soon there were more than 200 trouts and several thousand young salmon. All were fed with finely chopped sheep's liver. After three months, these fishlings were released into larger ponds, where they flourished and grew. In March 1865 most of the fish, five to six inches long, were liberated into the Plenty river, some in the Derwent and a few in the open sea. The hope was that these salmon would eventually return from the sea. But they did not. While the salmon disappeared, never to be seen again, the trout appeared to adapt well to local conditions.

By finally bringing trout to Tasmania over long years of experimentation fuelled by dogged determination, James Arndell Youl gave hope to his fellow colonials all over the Southern Hemisphere. He had proved that European brown trout could be acclimatized and domesticated in almost any cold water in the world.

Later, William Denison, James Youl and Frank Buckland were to all play important roles in the first serious attempt to acclimatize trout in India as well.

III

IT ALL BEGAN WITH FAILURE

IN 1855, WILLIAM DENISON, LIEUTENANT GOVERNOR OF what was no longer Van Diemen's Land but Tasmania, was promoted to governor and sent to New South Wales, a state on the east coast of Australia. There he spent six years as an administrator before being transferred to India in 1861, as governor of Madras in southern India. At this point, trout were still a few years away from arriving in Tasmania. But when Denison was transferred to India, he carried with him the dream of acclimatizing salmon and trout in a new land.

Madras Presidency was largely tropical, featuring high temperatures virtually through the year. The only exception was its hilly areas, especially the Nilgiris, the 'blue mountain' range that spans an area of 3,900 sq. km. At least 24 of the Nilgiris' peaks are above 6,600 ft, the highest being Doddabetta, at 8,652 ft.

By the time Denison became governor of Madras, the Nilgiris were already home to a set of hill stations popular among Europeans. For some they offered a quick weekend getaway, for others they afforded a longer holiday destination, and a few had even settled there permanently. By 1827, the Nilgiris' biggest town, Ootacamund or 'Ooty', had become the official sanatorium and summer capital of Madras Presidency.

Those who lived in the Nilgiris were experimenting with local flora and fauna, by acclimatizing new species. According to the *Nilgiri Guide and Directory* from 1916, 'Sir William Rumbold appears to have been the pioneer, when in 1830 he had fish from the plains placed in the Billikul lake near his bungalow at that place. In 1844 Mr. Martelli placed Carnatic carp in the same water. The Pykara river now holds good sport in its carp fishing.' Some settlers were eager to bring salmon and trout although they knew this would not be easy. In 1863, a certain Mr Thomas of the Madras Civil Services, tried to import 500 ova of (probably brown) trout, from Ripon in England. According to W. Francis's book *The Nilgiris* published in 1908, they were not kept sufficiently cool, and all the ova died before they reached Ceylon. Unfortunately, more details of this early effort are not available.

It was Dr Francis Day, assistant surgeon with the British Army, who made the first serious attempt to import trout eggs into India. Day's efforts are well recorded, thanks to the research done by P.J.P. Whitehead and P.K. Talwar, and published in the *Bulletin of the British Museum (Natural History)* in 1976.

Day, who is venerated as the 'father of Indian ichthyology', was a lean man with deep eyes and impressive eyebrows. He joined the East India Company in 1851. When Day sailed to India from Sussex, he did not have any interest in fishes. He wanted to study birds, as his hobby of choice was birdwatching. But these were no times for hobbies, as he was immediately sent to fight in the Second Burmese War. After spending many years with the army in Burma, he was posted back to mainland India. When the transfer of power from the East India Company to the Crown was taking place, Dr Day was transferred, first to Hyderabad and then to Cochin in 1859. It was here that he started to study the fishes of the Malabar area. He wrote a paper, 'The fishes of Cochin', in which he listed 211 fish species, and which earned him the fellowship of the Zoological Society of London. He now wanted to study the subject further.

In the summer of 1863, when Day was visiting the Nilgiris, he heard about Thomas's attempt to bring trout to India. Around the same time, Day received a small booklet titled *Fish Hatching*, written by his childhood friend Frank Buckland. Like Day, Buckland had joined the military as an assistant surgeon. But he later resigned and started collecting and hatching trout eggs. After reading about trout hatching, Day started to think seriously about introducing trout in the Nilgiris. He made a survey of the streams and rivers in these hills and decided that its water bodies offered a perfectly hospitable environment for trout.

The biggest problem was a familiar one – the distance from England. Day knew that only eyed ova could be transported. He also knew that ova hatch within 14 days, and that it took a ship at least 40 days to reach India, to which must be added a further three days for a rail and road journey to Ooty. But these constraints did not discourage Day from pursuing the project. Fortuitously, he was able to meet the governor of Madras, Sir William Denison, who told him to get in touch with James Youl.

When this meeting took place, Day was working simultaneously on two projects: attempting to stock trout in the Nilgiri Hills, and consolidating his work on the fishes of Cochin into a book. Both these projects necessitated a visit to England. Since he had the backing of the governor, Day's application for six months' leave was granted readily.

In England, Day was first entirely preoccupied with readying his book. Eventually, on 20 April 1864, he visited Youl in London. Here, Day saw ova of that were 93 and 143 days old, treated by ice, and surviving well. With the end of his leave imminent, he prepared a detailed plan for stocking the Nilgiri streams with trout and sent it to the Madras government. He was granted an extension of sick leave for a further six months. But for Day, this would not suffice. On 14 September, he wrote a letter to Governor Denison. He applied for an extension of one year, ostensibly claiming his recovery from illness was incomplete. But the same letter also made it clear that the extension was necessary for his trout project. The letter even had detailed suggestions on the subject – saying, for example, that the trout ova eggs had to be brought by a competent officer, that the eggs must be collected in winter, that the material can travel to India only in January or February, when the ships were less crowded, and so on. Governor Denison believed that Day was the right man for the project, and extended his leave by a year. In December, while still on leave, Day was promoted to the post of surgeon. Later in the same month, Day's book *Fishes of Malabar* was published by Cumberland House. He was now free to train all his energies on the trout project.

Day's extension was approved in the early part of 1865 and, by November 1865, he had acknowledged receipt of 60 pounds for the trout project from the Madras government. He then collected trout eggs for the Nilgiris in January 1866, planning to leave Southampton with the ova on 4 February 1866, sailing in a P and O steamer. He started negotiations over the supply of ice, especially for the difficult overland transfer by rail from the ship at Alexandria to a second ship at Suez (the Canal opened only three years later). Six stout boxes were procured. Three large slate troughs were then sent to Madras to receive the eggs.

Day then contacted his friend Frank Buckland for help and advice. The Hampshire streams around Southampton appeared ideal, being close enough to the port for the eggs to be brought to the ship easily. In early December, a friend of Day's at the Ordnance Survey Office invited him to view the trout stream. But the proprietors of the stream could not be persuaded to allow them to collect eggs. Eventually, he was given permission by Melville Portal, owner of the paper mill at Laverstoke Park near Micheldever in Hampshire (the Portals had for generations supplied the paper for Bank of England notes). Melville Portal was married to Lady Charlotte Mary, daughter of the Second Earl of Minto, whose father had been governor-general of India (1807–14). It is possible that Day may have known a member of the family in India, which helped him gain access to their influential and helpful English relatives.

On 18 January 1866, a very cold day, Day and Buckland set out for Laverstoke Park. On arriving, they immediately started to net the river Test in that particular stretch. In the beginning they caught only males or spent females, but Buckland, the expert, ensured that they collected thousands of trout eggs after a few hours. As mentioned by Whitehead and Talwar, it was a tiring experience for Day, who later wrote, 'It was raining incessantly all day (and) at 2.30 it become so cold from wading that I had to stop and to go for Red Lion [beer].' But Buckland enjoyed the experience, writing, 'I amazingly enjoy a day's trout egg collecting... it was a cold day, and I am as fond of cold as a polar bear.'

Buckland took a part of the collection to Windsor Park for his hatching experiment, and Day took the rest. The next morning he loaded his precious cargo onto the train to Southampton. The cans containing the eggs were slung on a stick across the seats. At the port these eggs, 6,000 in number, were packed in six pine boxes specially supplied by James Youl for the purpose. A layer of charcoal lined the bottom of each pine box, and the sides and bottom were perforated. The boxes were then put in the refrigeration room. When the ship *SS Mongolia* arrived on 2 February, the boxes were loaded onto the ship. The journey was circuitous; by ship to Alexandria, and then an overland journey by train to Suez. By the time these boxes reached Suez, nine tonnes of ice from the Wenham Lake Ice Company were ready and waiting. The boxes and ice were then loaded onto the *SS Bengal*.

The ship docked in Madras on 12 March. Day was satisfied, since everything had gone according to plan. Ahead lay a 450-km journey by train to Coimbatore (at the time the terminus of the railway). To protect the boxes from vibration, they were slung carefully from the roof of the carriage. When the boxes reached Coimbatore, Patrick Grant, the collector of the district, was there to receive them. Clearly, he was aware of the importance of the project and the governor's interest. The remaining 80 km to Ooty was accomplished on foot by a relay of bearers. In Ooty, a masonry hatching house had been built in the Government Garden according to instructions from Francis Day. The ova had stood the journey fairly well, the percentage of dead ranging only from 10 to 20.

Two months had now elapsed since Buckland and Day had collected the eggs. Day was anxious to see further results. All was going well but, suddenly, on 31 March a violent thunderstorm caused the water of the stream flowing through the hatching house to bring in silt and various insects. These insects began to devour the fish eggs. A long-cherished dream of the British in India and two years of hard work by Day had been undone by a single stray storm.

Two days later, Day was quoted in the local newspaper as saying that 'since Saturday afternoon (1 April) a very great mortality has set in amongst the trout eggs, as many as 300 having died that time'. Governor Denison himself visited the hatchery, the next day, where he saw the sad state of his pet project. For Denison, it was a second crushing failure, first in Australia and now in India. Not a single ovum hatched out. Day wrote letters to Youl and Buckland, but except for offering a few words of commiseration, they could do little to help him.

Almost immediately after this blow, Day received more bad news – his patron for the project, Governor William Thomas Denison, had returned to England. (As a tribute to this relationship, Day later bestowed on the beautiful barbel fish of Kerala the name Denison barb, or *Sahyadria denisonii*.)

When Francis Napier took charge as the Presidency's new governor, the dynamic changed completely. The new incumbent had no interest in Day's trout project. So Day decided to abandon the idea of trout acclimatization and turned his attention to bringing fishes up from the rivers of the plains. Meanwhile, some of his colleagues who had been critical about his 'long holiday' in the hills on government expenditure were determined to have him removed from the Nilgiris.

The latter half of 1866 saw a cholera outbreak across Madras Presidency, which eventually killed more than 100,000 people. This situation made it difficult for the government to indulge a trained medical practitioner's experiments with fish in faraway hills. Day was transferred to Kurnool (in present-day Andhra Pradesh). He was reluctant to go since his new project was in progress. The *Madras Times* demanded, 'Is this intended as a reward to the doctor for his eminent services in pisciculture?' The *Neilgherry Excelsior* was also critical: 'It was hoped that the endeavours of Dr Day to introduce low country fish [in the Nilgiris] would be supported – instead of this Lord Napier sends him down at once to a penal settlement.' Despite some fierce correspondence with the authorities, Day had no option but to leave the Nilgiri Hills.

However, after a brief period attending to medical matters, Day was reunited with his beloved fish. He wrote two volumes on fish in the *Fauna of British India, Including Ceylon and Burma* series published in 1889, where he gave details of more than 1,400 species. This pioneering work is still considered the bible of Indian ichthyology. Nor was his work on the trout project forgotten: In 1872, Day was awarded a silver medal by the Société D'Acclimatation of France in recognition of his herculean, though ultimately unsuccessful, efforts to establish trout in India.

Dr Francis Day had by now lost interest in trout acclimatization. But there were others who were as ready as he had been to take on the challenge. William Graham McIvor, superintendent of the government's cinchona plantation in the Nilgiris, was one such. This Scottish horticulturist was in charge of the Ooty Botanical Garden as well, having been tasked with transforming the wilderness into a beautiful 'English garden'. He did this successfully while also introducing a number of non-native plant species, including mulberry.

The cinchona plantation that McIvor supervised had an important place in the empire's scheme of things. In 1859, the British government had launched an expedition to South America with the aim of collecting seeds and plants of the quinine-producing cinchona tree to establish plantations in British India. Doing so would relieve the government of the escalating costs and uncertainties in the supply of this valuable anti-malarial drug. McIvor played a crucial role in establishing a plantation, and identified a site alongside the Dodabetta stream as suitable. It may have been that, walking round these cold and clear streams, he first thought about acclimatizing trout in the Nilgiris.

When McIvor was on leave, in England, he decided to bring back not only live trout but a number of other exotic fish. By now it had of course been well-established that transporting live trout was a highly challenging task, but McIvor was able to accomplish it innovatively and precisely. He gave an interesting account of his efforts in a government report dated 5 August 1869, where he recalled:

> I collected the live trout-fry in July 1867, and had them kept in an aquarium till the date of my departure to India,

to accustom them to the artificial conditions to which they would be subjected during the voyage. When first placed in the aquarium, a rapid flow of water was allowed to pass through it; after ten days this flow of water was gradually diminished; but as many of the fry died, the flow of the water was again increased, and continued for the next six weeks, when it again diminished with more favorable results. On leaving England I selected eighteen of the most healthy trout-fry to be conveyed to India. The other species of the fish had not this preparatory process, and I believe that this was a disadvantage. On 3rd November 1867, I left Southampton by P and O Steamer with eighteen lake Trout-fry, twenty four Tench, twelve Carp, twelve Rudd, twelve Silver Eels, and three Goldfish (one male and two female). Of those I succeeded in bringing to the Neilgherries, fifteen Trout, ten Carp, twenty four Tench, twelve Rudd, twelve Silver Eels and three Goldfish. The Gudgeon were all lost by an accident in the Red Sea; two trout were subsequently lost by leaping out of the tub in which they were placed; one female Goldfish died; nine Eels escaped into the running stream, and have not since been seen; the remaining three Eels were placed in a large pond in the gardens; and other species of fish in a house, or rather enclosure covered with wire-netting, specially prepared for their reception, by forming four ponds with a stream of clear water running through them. Previous to my departure I had the fry of each species placed separately in tin boxes 15x10 inches, fitted with small taps so as to

> allow [the] flow of water to pass from one box to other… The boxes should be placed in a wooden frame so as to stand one above the other. …The wooden frame should be slung or stand on the deck. It is better, however, that it should be slung, so as to swing to and fro with the motion of the ship. …The same arrangement should be adopted when conveyed by land in a railway carriage or otherwise. …The boxes are prepared for the reception of the fish by placing about 1/2 inch of well washed gravel at the bottom; they are then filled three parts full of water, and in this are placed a few aquatic plants to float in the water. These plants give off a small part of oxygen and afford shelter to the fish.

At the Nilgiri end of things, arrangements were made in the hatching house built for the ova transported by Dr Day in the Government Garden. McIvor reported to the government that these fishes were alive and healthy when they arrived. After a few months, he again reported that the fishes had been transferred to the Government Garden pond and that the trout, tench and rudd had spawned and there were 200 to 300 young fry, one or two inches in length. Funds were sanctioned immediately to distribute the fish in the various streams and other water bodies of the plateau region.

In August 1869 a formal ceremony was organized, at Ootacamund Lake. Lady Napier, wife of the governor, put the first set of fish in the lake. A superior gamefish from across the seas was finally testing Indian waters. McIvor himself placed the remaining fish in the Pykara and Avalanche rivers at Mukurthi, and in the Ootacamund, Burnfoot and Lovedale lakes.

Checking on the fish some months later, however, McIvor found that the little ones had not done well. Many had escaped down small nullahs and streams, presumed to have been caught with small nets by locals. Some had been captured as far down as the pool below the Kalhatti Falls. McIvor asked the government to provide protection for the fish from local fishermen who caught even the smallest fry, and destroyed them when they found they were worthless as food. To protect these 'superior' fishes a municipal by-law was framed. In *The Nilgiris* written by W. Francis in 1908, McIvor observed:

> No doubt, all our fishes are breeding rapidly, with the exception of trout; and the water of the hills will soon be alive with them. The trout also have produced young; and we caught some, but not nearly the number of the other kind. They, however, seems to be doing well in [the] Pykara and Macoorty streams, although I have not been able to catch any of them there. They should do well in Koondahas and the west side of the hills. The great quantity of mud washed in by heavy rain from the cultivated land in the east side of the hills will, I fear, render the stream unfit for trout.

After a few days, it was found that this experiment was not as successful as previously believed, even though some trout were said to have been afterwards caught in a stream near Naduvattam and six near the travellers' bungalow at Pykara (a common landmark). Despite its apparent failure, the project to bring trout into India attracted attention across the Western world. Thus, in its issue dated 22 November 1880, the *New York Times* wrote:

> Today a project is on foot to place English trout in the streams flowing from the Nilgiris, and should this be found possible, eventually other mountain rivers will be stocked. As in the higher regions of India the streams are all snow-fed, or arise from natural springs, there can be no reason why trout should not thrive there. The source of supply would probably be derived from New-Zealand, where trout has been introduced and the ova, properly packed, would be bought across the sea and transported to the Indian streams. It would, though, present no very great difficulty if California trout eggs were shipped from San Francisco. As the New-Zealand trout are of American parentage, the introduction of the fish in India would present a curious example of the distribution of aquatic life.

Gradually, interest in the matter began to wane. Even in 1886, when the success of the introduction of rainbow trout in Ceylon (now Sri Lanka) became worldwide news, there were few ripples of excitement in the Nilgiris.

However, some years later the Nilgiri Game Association picked up the project again with renewed zeal. Early in

1893, a lot of 40,000 ova were shipped but, when placed in the ice room of the steamer, froze to death. The next lot of 20,000 ova arrived in March. The weather, at that time, was too hot and nearly all died in consequence. Special arrangements were then made to receive future consignments. A fry pond and a stock pond were made at Marlimund Plantation near Snowdon House in Ooty, along with an elaborate series of seven fry ponds and a stock pond at Pykara. Later a hatchery was also made at Shola. The man at the helm of these efforts was Major General Rhodes Morgan, honorary secretary of the association.

Between 1893 and 1897, a series of consignments of trout ova of various kinds, both English brown trout and American rainbow trout, were imported and hatched with varying degrees of success. Hundreds of trout were placed in the Pykara, Avalanche, Emerald Valley and Kundah rivers, in the Burnfoot lake, the Marlimund and Dodabetta reservoirs, and the Snowdon pond. When in 1902, a 7lb trout was killed at the Emerald Valley stream, a great deal was written about it. But this turned out to be a flash in the pan. Thus, when a certain Major Bagnell of the Yorkshire Regiment came to the Nilgiris on an angling trip, he was deeply disappointed. In an article for F. G. Aflalo's book *The Sportsman's Book For India* published in 1904, he wrote, 'Trout have been imported here for some years, and have been put into most rivers and lakes. We only know of Salmo frio and of these there are many survivors of large size – up to 7 lbs. Female fish in spawn are often seen, but I have seen neither milting males nor small fry.

... The big trout I have caught have been sluggish and give little sport.' Writing in 1908 of these experiments, the *Madras District Gazetteer* remarked that 'though the fish put down lived and throve in some cases, the temperature of the water was too high for them to breed in successfully, for when it rises above 60* F, the ova for the brown and rainbow trout hatch out so quickly that the alevins are too weak to survive.'

Those who had tried so hard to plant trout in the streams of the Nilgiris in the second half of the nineteenth century were hobbyists and enthusiasts, none of them experts in trout planting or breeding. What they had in abundance was time and passion. And the colonial government was always ready to provide financial support. So while it cannot be said that the trout-breeding efforts had succeeded in any definitive way, they were not to be dismissed altogether. It was thus that, with the optimism of the true sportsman, Maj. Bagnell of the Yorkshire Regiment remarked: 'I am convinced that rainbow trout will yet succeed [in the Nilgiris].'

IV

TROUT IN THE KASHMIR VALLEY

TWO THOUSAND FIVE HUNDRED MILES NORTH OF THE Nilgiris, in the beautiful valley of Kashmir, it is always cool and often very cold. Unlike the Nilgiris, where all the water bodies are fed by springs or episodic rainfall, most of the rivers and streams in the Kashmir valley, like European streams, are snowfed. So it was natural to think that the Valley would provide the best environment in India for trout acclimatization, its cold weather and abundant water enabling the fish of the Salmo family to reproduce its kind unhindered.

Across India, the British had built upland holiday destinations for recreation and relief from the hot weather of the plains. But Kashmir, the valley beyond the Pir Panjal mountain range, had a special place in their hearts. For one, its scenery was grand beyond imagination. For another, the place looked and felt like Europe to the nostalgic colonial. When Francois Bernier, a French physician and traveller, visited Kashmir in 1665, he compared it to Switzerland. Two-and-a-half centuries later, when Lt. Col. Alban Wilson of the 8th Gurkha Rifles visited with his wife, Kashmir reminded him of Germany. As Wilson later wrote in his famous book, *Trout Fishing in Kashmir* published in 1920: 'We were both struck by the resemblance of Srinager to some parts of Germany: the roads lined with poplars, the architecture of the European houses, the orchard with their regular rows of apple and other fruit trees, the cornfield without fences, and even the style, not to mention the smell of the surrounding country villages.' The only thing missing in this 'Indian Europe' was trout. His description of the streams of Kashmir tells us a lot about his passion:

> The main river of Kashmir is Jhelum, but draining into it are numerous offshoots and streams, which take their source from the snow-fed hilltops, and gathering strength, they change from mountain torrent to stream, and, following through the foothills, join the mother river slowly passing through the valley. These streams are such as to delight the heart of a fisherman, here a foaming torrent breaking into the long deep pool, there a bank of weed with a clear patch of water, which seems to ask for a dry fly to be floated over it; again a meeting of the waters, which might hold a thirty pound salmon…

Given raptures such as these, why then was the idea of bringing trout to India conceived in the Nilgiris and not in Kashmir?

The princely state of Jammu and Kashmir had its own set of problems. When the great king of Kashmir, Maharaja Gulab Singh, founder of the Dogra dynasty, died in 1857, the pundits of the court informed his son, the new Maharaja, that the soul of his father had entered the body of a *chiru*, the Himalayan trout, and was swimming in the streams of his kingdom. So Ranbir Singh, the new maharaja, issued an edict prohibiting the killing of any fish in all of the state, to safeguard the everlasting bliss of Gulab Singh's soul.

However, Kashmir's was a meat-eating society, and fish was an essential part of the Kashmiri diet. Within a few years of this edict, two famines struck, in 1878 and 1887, respectively. The Maharaja had no option but to lift the ban. Yet, even after the ban was lifted, no one was allowed to catch fish between Amiran Kadal and Zaina Kadal, the first and second city bridges in Srinagar.

After the ban on killing fish was lifted, it was time to think of introducing trout in Kashmir. Among the first to pursue the idea seriously was Walter R. Lawrence, the state's settlement commissioner. In his book *The Valley of Kashmir* published in 1895, he wrote, 'The rainbow trout of Canada, used to snow water, might very easily be introduced into Kashmir. And the Talbel valley, when the waterworks reservoir is completed, would be a very suitable place for the experiment.' In *The Sportsman's Book for India* by F. G. Aflalo published in 1904, Col. Unwin likewise wrote, 'I would suggest that the rainbow trout of Canada and America would be more suitable than the

English trout, as being more used to snow-water...Pike might also be tried in the Dal and Manasbal lakes, and small detached lakes near Sambal.'

Also interested in introducing trout into Kashmir was Frank James Mitchell, an officer of Scottish origin who returned to the Valley many years after his retirement. During his career as an officer in Kashmir, Mitchell had not been interested in fish or fishing. His hobby of choice was golf. After retiring in May 1890, he spent nine years in his native Scotland, which is where his interest in angling was kindled. Scotland's streams were abrim with trout and Mitchell learnt a lot about these spotted beauties.

Frank Mitchell was living a retired life in Scotland with his wife and three children, after having invested all his savings in South African mines. But suddenly the South African bubble burst and he was left with no money at all. It was the beginning of a difficult time for a man who had spent many years in safe and leisurely conditions. His younger brother William Mitchell was at the time running a carpet factory and a road construction firm in Srinagar. When William heard about his brother's misfortune, he immediately invited Frank to move to Kashmir. Frank was at first hesitant but after his wife died he decided to join his brother in India.

In 1899, Frank Mitchell arrived in Kashmir to help run his brother's carpet factory at Bagh-e-Dilawar Khan. After just a few months, he produced a new kind of dye which was of great value to the carpet industry. But destiny had other plans for him.

On his first holiday, Frank took his fishing gear to the Arrah river, a tributary of the reservoir at Harwan, famous for its magnificent garden and a Buddhist stupa. The river, the atmosphere, the scenery were all perfect but, alas, there were no trout. A day's disappointing angling made Frank wistfully recall the brown trout of Scotland. The thought struck him that if the local fish '...could be replaced by the beauties I had loved at home, here was indeed a true angler paradise,' as mentioned in 'How Trout Were Introduced Into Kashmir' by Mitchell, in the *Journal of Bombay Natural History Society* in 1926.

Frank then discussed the idea of importing trout with his brother William, who was also very keen to see trout in these streams. So was the well-known sportsman Col. A.E. Ward, who was an active member of the Bombay Natural History Society. Col. Unwin and a Capt. Allan were also brought on board. These sportsmen formed the Kashmir Fishing Club with the primary purpose of introducing salmon and trout in the Valley. Frank Mitchell was elected secretary. A corpus fund was formed with several individual donations of £50 each. To begin with, this was a completely private project, with no official grant either from the Durbar at Srinagar or from the British government.

Fortuitously, Frank Mitchell met a British official seconded to the Maharaja. Maj. Godfrey told him that the Duke of Bedford wanted to do something for Kashmir in return for the stags presented to him by the Durbar. The Duke would be pleased to send trout ova if someone would commit to do the work necessary to establish the fish in Kashmir. Frank volunteered immediately. In preparation for receiving the trout ova he established a small hatchery, breeding local fishes to begin with. Here he gave lessons in fertilizing ova and stripping fish to his faithful henchman Sodahma (Sudama) Pandit. Of his Kashmiri assistant, Frank wrote: 'He was openly incredulous of the result when I told him to put them (the oreinus fertilized ova) into the hatching box and it was evidently with new respect that he came some days later to tell me they all hatched out.' Sodahma was to become key to the propagation of trout in north India. While the Kashmiri was learning the tricks of fish hatching, Frank was busy studying the life of local insects, toads, leeches, large water beetles and their larvae.

Meanwhile, he discovered that someone had already brought trout ova to north India. This was Capt. S.D. Kitcher of the 5th Gorkha Rifles, posted at Abbottabad (the same town that made contemporary international headlines when American Navy SEAL commandos killed Osama Bin Laden of the extremist organization Al-Qaeda more than a hundred years later). In 1895–96, Capt. Kitcher tried to hatch ova in the swimming pool of his regimental club at Abbottabad. When he found the ova dying, he threw them into the nearby Kalapani stream, believing that his efforts had failed entirely. He later discovered that these ova had in fact hatched in the beautiful hilly stream and that some fish had survived. The eggs might have died for lack of oxygen in the swimming pool and actually flourished in the natural stream where they got fresh oxygenated water. Capt. Kitcher sent notes of his findings to Frank Mitchell in a letter dated 30 June 1900. 'At the beginning of this month I was at Abbottabad,' he wrote, 'and while I was there, some fish were seen in part of our water, of which five were caught and put back again. The biggest one was 14 inches long and must have weighed about 1½ lbs. These fish have bred (for the last two years, I think). I mention this as I have no doubt it will interest you.'

In Abbottabad, another attempt was made by a man in the same regiment – Lt. Col. Kemball, who restocked this stream. Those trout did well for the first few years, before being killed off by Gurkha sepoys. Meanwhile, Frank got a letter from Maj. Godfrey suggesting that the shipment of ova from England should synchronize with the melting of snow on the Rawalpindi–Srinagar Road. (Incidentally, this road was constructed by William Mitchell's firm, with the project supervised by another brother, Harry.) Sadly, when the ova sent by the Duke of Bedford finally arrived on the Indian coast, none were alive. For the shipment had been made on a steamer with no cooling room.

Frank Mitchell and his mate Maj. Godfrey were undeterred by this failure. Godfrey travelled to England from where he arranged a fresh lot of ova from Howietown. This time the consignment was shipped on a P and O mail steamer named *Caledonia*, which had a well-equipped cooling room.

The steamer docked at Bombay port in December 1900. The long journey from Bombay to Srinagar lay ahead, first by train and then by road. A man named J. Sidgreaves Macdonald had already been sent to Bombay to receive the ova. When he was on his way back, snowfall on the Srinagar Road threatened the safe passage of the eggs, but fortunately they made it before the road closed.

It was Christmas week and most of the English officers were busy with festivities. But Frank Mitchell was waiting for his prize guests, the thousands of trout ova from Scotland. The arrangements for receiving and housing them had been made in the veranda of his residence. It was late evening of 19 December when Macdonald arrived with the packed ova. Frank spent much of the night washing and transferring the eggs to hatching boxes. Frank was pleased with the condition of the ova, about 6,000 of which appeared to be healthy.

Just as Frank Mitchell thought everything was going according to plan, the municipal water supply to his house stopped. Frank realized that his decision to use piped water supply for trout hatching had been injudicious. Every time the town's water supply failed, he had to deploy his men to carry water from a nearby stream. Because of this perhaps, the mortality rate was higher at the alevin and fry stages. But the advantage was that there was no danger of attack by insects and leeches.

Soon, the ova hatched and little fish emerged. In February, some were transferred into the fry pond excavated in the compound of the Mitchell residence. In this fry pond the fish were hand-fed, mostly by Sohdama. Some fish were sent to Gupkar, an irrigation canal above the Harwan. The canal was netted at both ends to prevent the fish escaping or from being attacked by carnivorous fish. No more hand-feeding here; now they had to rely on nature and their own resources. After some days, Frank measured the size of the yearlings. He was happy to find one fish larger than ten and a half inches, at that time a record for a yearling of its age. The yearlings in the Gupkar canal measured about five inches. The difference perhaps owed to Sohdama's careful feeding. Now Frank was confident that his project would indeed succeed.

The original plan was that the state would lease the Arrah river and some other streams to the fishing club, but when the time to transfer the little fish came, the British Resident to the Maharaja worried that giving the river to private hands would set a poor precedent. He suggested the establishment of a game preservation department to run the venture. When this department was founded, Frank Mitchell was made its honorary director and Maj. H.R. Wingram its secretary. The fishing club was then abolished.

It was time to transfer these yearlings. By October 1900, a stock pond was ready at Dachigam Rukh (now a part of Dachigam National Park). Some yearlings were transferred to this pond, some placed in the Panchgam pond and the rest sent to the Arrah river, five miles up from Harwan. By this time the money raised by Frank Mitchell from the initial subscriptions was about to run out. The Resident in Kashmir, Col. Harold Deane, was approached but he declined to help. Fortunately, Deane was soon succeeded by a more sympathetic man,

Sir Louis Dane. Frank Mitchell took the new Resident to Panchgam, equipped with his fly rod. The Resident dropped the first artificial fly into the stock pond, and a yearling obligingly emerged to be caught. Within a few days a sum of Rs 2,000 was disbursed. The project was back on track. In a few months the yearlings started to develop into adult trout.

However, just as Frank and his mates thought they had successfully introduced trout in Kashmir, the great flood of 1903 swept over the Valley. In July, the Arrah breached its banks and the water carried away the stockpond and scattered the trout. Frank stoically waited for the flood to subside. But when the waters receded he was surprised to find that trout had enjoyed the flood thoroughly. Not even one remained in the pond. They had settled in holes and pools at different locations, which they seemed to find greatly to their liking. It was decided not to disturb them. The spawning season was at hand. Most of the trout had already selected a shallow gravel (known as redds) which received a more forceful flow of water and hence greater supply of oxygen, for themselves and also for their young ones. By the summer of 1904, a well-populated new generation of trout were found in the streams. At long last, it appeared that trout could not merely survive but also thrive in this part of India.

This was good news for everybody, even for the Kashmir Durbar. The Durbar now offered to construct a new hatchery at Harwan outside the Rukh. The hatchery was placed near two springs that supplied water generously, and had tanks above for young fish and below for breeding fish. Another consignment of ova of brown trout and rainbow trout was arranged from Scotland to stock the new hatchery. A new stock pond was also built at Achabal.

Despite all these happy developments, the successful acclimatization of trout in Kashmir was at first not widely known or accepted among Europeans in India. Those who had heard of the failures of Francis Day and others in the Nilgiris were not convinced that this experiment would last. Nor was there any public announcement about this project, perhaps because the streams of Kashmir were not adequately stocked. In the last week of June 1905, the new Resident, Colonel Pears, and his wife visited to check the progress of the project in the Rukh. The stream was full, since it was summer and the snow was melting rapidly. After lunch they went to the stream above the Panchgam pond. When they caught nine little trout, and also saw a very big trout at the old temple pool below, the Pears were impressed. But a few days later Mrs Pears told Frank Mitchell with some deprecatory amusement that when she talked about her experience at the Rukh, one gentleman had remarked, 'Oh! Mitchell just catches the same trout over and over again to make you think there are lots of them.'

The next month Frank told his brother William about the big trout he had seen. On 9 July, William and four friends went to the point where the big trout had been spotted. A perfect 5 lb cock fish fell victim to a fly spoon. They cooked it for lunch and the exciting news travelled swiftly. Sportsmen from all over India started to arrive for fishing holidays. In October 1906, the viceroy of India, Gilbert John Elliot-Murray-Kynynmound, 4th Earl of Minto, visited Kashmir. He had the pleasure of seeing, and later eating, a male trout weighing 12 lb and measuring 27 inches from nose to tail and with a girth of 18 inches. The fish had grown twenty-five times in a two-year period.

Some years later a news story appeared in *The Pioneer*, headlined 'A Record Trout'. The correspondent wrote, 'While fishing in the river Bringhy, Kashmir, on 22nd May, Mr. Percy Brown succeeded in landing a magnificent trout, weighing 14 pounds, its length being 31 inches and girth 19 inches. The fish undoubtedly constitute the record for Kashmir, and probably for India, as heretofore the largest trout captured has not exceeded 10 pounds. The fish was caught on an artificial minnow, and put up a good fight before it was eventually grassed.' When popular journals began to send correspondents to Kashmir, to cover fishing expeditions and to publish detailed articles on this new recreation, it was clear that the trout project was a success.

Meanwhile, Frank Mitchell continued his efforts to make Kashmir a home for trout. In 1905 he began preparations for artificial spawning, seeking to emulate the best trout farms in England and Scotland. For he well knew how expensive and tortuous the whole process of getting ova from home every year was: procuring the eggs, finding suitable steamers with adequate cold storage, making arrangements for a long and difficult land journey from Bombay to Kashmir, by unreliable train and even less reliable cart. But for this new experiment to succeed he needed more funds. On 9 January 1906, Mitchell wrote a long, impassioned letter to Sir Louis Dann, Secretary in the foreign department (and former Resident of Kashmir), pleading for governmental assistance:

> The flood of 1903 swept over my ponds at Panchgam and all the stock trout escaped into the river. They have, however, taken good care of themselves and have bred and multiplied under natural conditions beyond my sanguine hopes. This once [and] for all settles the vexed question as to whether trout once released into the Himalayan streams can hold their own. Their success has been amazing.
>
> But their escape left me without any stock trout with which to complete the experiment. Our primary object was, of course, to stock the Kashmir rivers and lakes, more with a view to benefit the disciple of Izak Walton. This, however, is a narrow and rather selfish aim: the true objective should be, in my opinion, to prove that a trout farm capable of supplying and stocking all the streams and lakes of Himalayas can be established in Kashmir, and if properly managed, made into a sound commercial undertaking.
>
> I had to begin again. A fresh lot of ova was imported and new stock ponds were made: this time at Harwan, below the reservoir, as there were objections to the

former site inside the Rukh. Funds only permitted of my starting three small ponds, each 50'x4'x4', sufficient for an experiment, but not for a business undertaking.

Mitchell continued:

> The question is whether the Government of India are disposed to interest themselves in the development of trout culture. The subject of pisciculture is one which has been earnestly taken up by the Government of nearly all our colonies and in America and on the Continent. It occurs to me that the matter is one which should concern the Government of India even to a greater extent, for fish form a more important item of diet amongst the natives of India than it does in any other of England's dependencies. The attitude of the Kashmir Government is one of stolid indifference, inclining to hostility on account of the supposed transmigration of the soul of the former ruler to Kashmir fish. Imported fish are consequently regarded with suspicion.

This letter was followed by a chain of correspondence between different officials and Mitchell. All to no avail, as the government finally declined to fund the project.

Meanwhile, the hatchery at Harwan and the stock pond at Achabal were ready for the further propagation of trout. But neither Frank nor his locally trained workers had any experience of how to proceed. Frank made an artificial spawning bed with a wire net trap for ova. Within a few days he had collected around 2,000 ova from the net, but only 900 proved fertile and hatched out. Unfortunately, a water shrew got into the box one night and ate almost all the little alevins. Now there was no option but to wait for the next spawning season.

From the following year, nothing went wrong. The progress was so remarkable that, by 1908, Frank Mitchell and his men started to collect more than one million eyed ova annually. It was now possible to stock all the streams of Kashmir and Gilgit. Trout was thus acclimatized over almost the entire territory of Kashmir. In Vishnu, Kishanganga, Istahal and Kulgam, trout frolicked in virtually every stream and pool of the princely state. All these rivers, streams and pools were thoroughly mapped and named. In the introduction to Lt. Col. Alban Wilson's *Trout Fishing in Kashmir* published in 1920, Maj. H.R. Wingram, secretary of the Game Preservation Department, gave details of the propagation. He wrote:

> The first river to be stocked was the Arrah or Dachigam stream flowing through the state preserve of that name... In 1906, followed the Achbal, which comes hurtling and rushing from half a dozen springs from under the Achbal hill and then flows like an English trout stream, through green meadows and rice fields, till it joins the Jhelum near Islamabad. ...The Veshau, with its two branches Istahal and Kulgam, or Tehsil, quickly followed and I shall always remember the joy with which I saw, in the autumn of 1908, a 2½ pounder taken on a fly by

Mr. J.H. Phelps... The Kishanganga and its tributary at Burdwan is now a typical dry fly stream, which yields fish upto three pounds. These afford grand sport, when you consider the tiny flies and the finest gut are necessary in the still clear water of the river.

In the same year, the Bringi was started. Seven hundred yearlings were put down from the hatcheries at Achbal, in the upper water, near the game preservation sanctuary at Rajparan, followed next year by two thousand more fry, and in September, 1910 I tried this part of the river and took fish of sixteen, fifteen, fourteen inches, etc. From this time on, stocking was continued, both by ova from Harwan and fry from Achbal, and the Bringi is now full of magnificent trout...

The later rivers to be taken in hand are Madmati, a grand stream which joins the Woolar lake at Bandipur...; the Erin, which has so far not fulfilled the promise I hoped for, the Wangat which drains the snowclad slopes of Haramook...; the Thricker, a branch of Liddar, and the Nowboog, a tributary of Bringi, and lastly the high lake of Gangabal, which prove that an altitude of some 12,000 feet is no handicap to the welfare of brown trout.

Stocking trout at Gilgit – almost 200 miles away from the Valley, and approached over a treacherous mountainous road, across a number of smaller valleys and high passes – proved most difficult. The greatest challenge was preventing ova from freezing in this snowbound region.

But the challenge was conquered: two army officers stationed there, Col. A.B. Dew and Col. Macpherson, were so enthusiastic about the experiment that they built a hatchery at their own expense. But trout stocked in Gilgit was never as abundant as in the Valley.

Frank Mitchell also tried to stock the high lakes of Kashmir with trout. These lakes, too, were frozen over even as late as June and success here was as partial as in Gilgit. Frank next chose to take trout beyond Kashmir, to the whole Himalayan and sub-Himalayan region. In any case, enquiries were pouring in. British officers were keen to have these European beauties in their own particular local streams. Ova had already been sent to Abbottabad, Nainital, Shillong, Shimla, Kangra and Kullu. The most successful experiment was in the Kullu valley, aided by Frank's assistant Sodahma.

In 1908, Mitchell expanded the scope of his experiment even further. He imported the ova of Danube Salmon (*S. hucho*). According to his paper in the *Journal of the Bombay Natural History Society*, a 'well known continental pisciculturist' shipped these ova from London to Calcutta. When the consignment arrived in April, Mitchell personally went to collect and bring the ova to Kashmir. But the trout from these ova were not as healthy as previous batches. When Mitchell complained, an inquiry found that since the guaranteed ova from the government hatchery were not available, late salmon ova from a private hatchery had been sent in their stead. Cecil Lang aka 'Skene Dhu' had a different disparaging explanation for this failure. He wrote, 'Regarding the "Salmo Huchen" the less said about these the better; they were shipped by a German, which explain[s] everything, and none are in existence in the vale.'

Mitchell also wished to introduce rainbow trout in Manasbal lake. In 1904, he imported a small quantity of rainbow trout ova, but none hatched out. Later, in 1912, his Calcutta-based friend, W.W. Petrie, imported 1,000 rainbow trout alevins from Britain and had them shipped in a P and O mail steamer. Petrie also arranged to have the alevin delivered successfully to Harwan. These dwindled to a very small number before they reproduced their kind, but eventually a fair stock was established. Although by this time rainbow trout had already been established in the streams of Nilgiris, Kashmir was the only place in India where one could kill both forms of trout.

The indefatigable Frank Mitchell next tried to cross-breed these varieties of trout, but the results were unsatisfactory. However, such failures were trifling in comparison to his remarkable achievements in introducing trout to India. As Lt. Col. Wilson wrote in his 1920 book *Trout Fishing in Kashmir*:

> I would remark that one could fish all over the United Kingdom with infinitely less chances of success in getting a really big river trout, (that is, one of eight pounds or more) that one has doing so in Kashmir, and would probably have to pay a good deal more for the permission to try and catch him, if the river was

> preserved. Anyone who is keen on trout fishing, and does not wish to kill more trout then he needs for his own and his friends' consumption, could not do better than give Kashmir a trial.

While Mitchell's pioneering efforts gave a lot to Kashmir, to its rivers and to the British in India, he himself received little financial recognition or assistance. His efforts to get government help had been in vain. Nonetheless the entrepreneur in him decided to launch a new and quite different venture: he started an olive plantation in Punjab's Attock district. He imported Italian trees, which initially did very well, but then the project foundered. In 1920, he ventured into yet another field, taking 700 acres of land on lease from the Punjab government and undertaking to grow grapes and produce dried raisins and currants. This was followed by a citrus plantation.

By now his sons had joined him from Scotland to work in his various businesses. The Mitchell family ventured into processed food under two brand names, Kissan and Mitchell's. Kissan is still a popular food brand in India; in 1950 the original owners, the Mitchells, sold it to Vitthal Mallya of the UB group, and a few decades later it was bought by the multinational giant Unilever. In present-day Pakistan, though, Mitchell's remains a leading food brand; a company named Mitchell's Fruit Farms Ltd is still based in Attock, although its ownership is now in local hands.

For all this entrepreneurial success, though, Frank James Mitchell's greater glory lies in the years and effort he devoted to his passion for establishing trout in Kashmir. Certainly, that work enhanced Kashmir's status as a major tourist attraction for the next few decades. Mitchell's contribution was perhaps best described by the diplomat and sportsman Philip K. Crowe. In 1955, when Crowe was American ambassador to Ceylon, he visited Kashmir with his wife and daughter, solely to fish for trout. Writing about his visit in the 53rd volume of the *Journal of the Bombay Natural History Society* published in 1955, he remarked:

> It was difficult to improve on the fabulous Himalayan pleasure land of Kashmir, but two men succeeded in doing it. The Mogul Emperor Jehangir built the lovely Shalimar [Gardens], and an Englishman named Mitchell imported brown trout. The result is that today one can wander among the flowers and fountains of the famous garden by the Dal Lake or, as I prefer, angle along some of the world's most sporting and spectacular, streams and rivers.

V
TROUT IN CEYLON

THE SUCCESS OF THE TROUT PROJECT IN KASHMIR WAS a matter of joy and pride for many Europeans in India. However, white settlers in the Nilgiris were more interested in the success of trout culture in Ceylon (now Sri Lanka) just across the sea, a land that was closer geographically, topographically and culturally. The experiment of trout acclimatization in Ceylon started much later than in the Nilgiris, but succeeded even before it did in Kashmir.

Ceylon, an island with lofty mountains, luxuriant forests and beautiful beaches, had long been attractive to Europeans. Its climate is generally tropical and warm, with the exception of the cool central highlands. The coolest place in these hills is Nuwara Eliya (6,128 ft), which is blessed with a picturesque landscape and a number of crystal clear streams in its vicinity. The establishment of commercial tea farming in and around Nuwara Eliya enhanced its importance. The owners and managers of the tea estates were European settlers, all rendered unhappy by the absence of their favourite sport. After the success of the trout experiment in Tasmania, they too started to dream about importing trout into Ceylon.

Hugh L. Hubbard, a planter of St. Johns Estate, Uda Pussellawa, was the first to make the attempt. This was in 1880, several years after Francis Day's efforts in India. Unfortunately, there are only scanty records of Hubbard's experiment. We know that he imported ova in two batches, each containing 15,000 eggs. A 1912 article by Col. W. Molesworth and J. Bryant in the *Journal of the Bombay Natural History Society* remarked:

> The ova, which resemble delicate pink peas, were packed with the greatest care, in alternate layers, between moss, and were protected with a covering of muslin which prevented the eggs from escaping or being crushed. They were then placed on zinc trays, which were enclosed in a box. This box was put inside a larger box, and was surrounded by charcoal. Ice was kept constantly on the package, and the temperature was never allowed to rise above 40°. The hatching progress was thus retarded, or suspended, during the journey. As soon as the ova arrived at Nuwara Eliya they were placed in hatching tanks, and immediately the little fish began to appear, all eyes and tail, and none the worse for their travels in the embryo state.

Hubbard placed 20 brown trout (*Salmo fario*) into the Nuwara Eliya stream. Others were put into the dam at Oliphant Estate. The journal further informs us that 'the little fish were carried from their nursery in Nuwara Eliya in old kerosene tins, slung on a pole, and borne by two coolies. Every twenty minutes the water was aerated by means of a syringe, a process which the fry enjoyed immensely, if one may judge by the way in which they clustered under the jet of air.' The initial growth of these fishes in the dam was recorded. It was slow, with trout attaining the weight of 3 lb in 18 months. (But much later, in 1904, when a fish of 14 lb was captured in the lake, it became clear that the experiment had been successful.)

Meanwhile, in 1882, when news of trout being placed in Nuwara Eliya got around, it was welcomed enthusiastically by the European community. A Trout Fund Committee was formed to fund future attempts. European planters and civilians donated liberally for the purpose. By 1888, Rs 27,000, a considerable sum at the time, had been collected for the introduction of brown trout and rainbow trout (*Salmo iridens*). An individual's effort soon became a community's obsession. Consignments of different varieties of trout ova started to arrive at different ports of Ceylon even as hatcheries were being built. Dreams of having trout in the hilly streams of this beautiful island started converting into reality. There are numerous records of such import. In 1890, Wilson Wood imported frio ova, and in 1891 Andrew of Guildford sent out 3,000 ova. Then there was a George Fowler who imported 22,000 frio ova.

The news of trout acclimatization of trout in Ceylon started to appear in the international media, though accompanied by somewhat deprecating comments. An item in a newspaper in New Zealand, published in July 1894, remarked: 'We noticed in the Ceylon "Times" that trout have been successfully acclimatized in streams on the high lands of the Island of Ceylon. Specimens of 5lbs weight have been taken. We should think that in such a climate the trout would soon lose its originally fine flavour. It has deteriorated in New Zealand.'

However, available records have only a few of tales of angling. These tell us that in November 1894, a 7-pounder was caught in the stream, and a few months later, an 8-pounder. In early 1898, a huge brown trout of 9 lb was caught.

At a public meeting of the Trout Fund Committee held on 18 January 1896, it was decided to convert the organization into a full-fledged Ceylon Fishing Club, as mentioned in *The Fishing Gazette*, with an aim 'to stock the streams and lakes of Ceylon with trout and other suitable fish that afford good sport, and to regulate the fishing of such streams and lakes as may be stocked'. The government leased to the club fishing rights in all waters above 4,000 ft, for a token 'annual sum of Rs 100, *viz.*, Rs 50 for water within the Local Board limit of Nuwara Eliya, Rs 25 for water in the Central Province outside Local Board limits, and Rs 25 for the water in the Sabaragamuwa'.

Soon the club started to make money from fishing licences. The cost of fishing was Rs 30 per subscriber. But the club also suffered heavy losses because of high import costs. It then began to think of breeding the fish locally. By 1899, though, it became quite clear that breeding brown trout in Ceylon was far from easy. According to the book *Diversions of a Diplomat in Ceylon* by Philip K. Crowe published in 1956:

> Careful observation at the hatchery indicated, in fact, that the hen and the cock brown trout seldom came in season at the same time. The brown trout, furthermore, were inveterate cannibals and tended to decimate their own ranks. Mr. Lushington, in one of his early reports, stated that he left four small fish of about two inches each in one of the troughs of the hatchery. Ten days later he found that one of these trout had grown to three inches while the others had vanished, ostensibly down the gullet of their voracious companion. ...In an attempt to import a fish that would breed in Ceylon waters and be less prone to cannibalism, it was decided to experiment with rainbows.'

The Ceylon Fishing Club then decided to turn its attention exclusively to rainbow trout. After two years of efforts, the first country-bred trout were seen in Ceylon. It was a magical moment for the island's European community. In 1902, a large number of locally bred trout, 4 to 6 inches long, were observed in the Nuwara Eliya and Horton plain streams. And by 1903 it was quite apparent that the country-bred fish had themselves propagated their species.

The next step for the Fishing Club was to take proper advantage of this success. It was decided to get an expert pisciculturist from England to construct a hatchery and to start artificial breeding of trout. To secure the services of this expert, money was raised by issuing debentures. In May 1905, A.E. Armstrong, a well-known pisciculturist of Cardiff in Wales, came to join the Ceylon Fishing Club as its superintendent, bringing with him considerable experience and a diploma from the Royal Aquarium. He was also an honorary officer of the Thames Angling Association. But the troubled man attempted suicide within a few weeks of his arrival in Ceylon and died on June 3 while in hospital.

A search for another expert began immediately. A few weeks after Armstrong's death, another Englishman, H.C. Wilson, was chosen as his replacement. In his first report Wilson wrote, as quoted from Cecil Lang's 1923 book *The Mighty Mahseer and Other Fish*:

> Salmo fario breeds in Ceylon are beyond any question. The reason there are so few is owing to the great mortality during the alevin stage. The temperature of the water hatches the egg so rapidly that the young fish perish through weakness, only an occasional one surviving.

This closed the chapter of brown trout in Ceylon.

Wilson's report also noted that the worst enemy of trout in Ceylon were native poachers. Their practice of using basket traps, set-lines and poison were killing trout in large numbers. Wilson himself caught two such poachers and handed them over to the police, a magistrate then issuing a punishment of ten lashes each.

According to Crowe:

> Studying cannibalism in trout, Wilson came to the conclusion that they bred abnormally fast in Ceylon and in this process developed unusually large heads. Later, when the trout started to decline, owing to old age, the thinning body appeared out of all proportion to the head and it was during this shrinking period that the trout turned cannibal. By inspecting the gullets of trout of this odd appearance, he found a far higher percentage of cannibal remains than in the normal trout.

Further, when Wilson studied the food habits of Ceylon trout, he found that they ate mainly crabs, shrimps, worms, beetles and snails and larvae of different flies. It was also found that Ceylon trout seldom rose to local flies. George Fowler suggested that English mayflies be imported to tempt them. Since the craze for trout fishing was intensifying by the day, a large shipment of mayflies was made from England, but to no avail. Soon Wilson found some local flies which were more acceptable to Ceylon trout.

He then started a project for the artificial spawning of rainbow trout in Ceylon. In 1910, the first ova were successfully taken from local rainbow trout. This opened the door to a number of possibilities. The Ceylon Fishing Club became independent of imports to stock its streams. It also enabled the club to export the ova to India and Burma.

VI

TROUT FINALLY COMES TO THE NILGIRIS

IN THE NILGIRI HILLS, TROUT LOVERS HAD BEEN WATCHING the experiment in Ceylon closely, for the struggle to establish this fish in peninsular India continued. Trout ova were being imported regularly, with small spurts of success and greater bouts of failure. Cecil Lang gave an interesting account of these efforts in the *Tropical Agriculturist and Magazine of the Ceylon Agricultural Society*, writing:

> The first lot was entrusted to some genius who was possessed of a little knowledge which is so dangerous a thing. Trout ova he had them stowed in the refrigerating room of the steamer which brought them out where they straight[a]way froze to death. The next lot were sent out so that they arrived in the middle of the hot weather, and they were roasted to death. Yet another lot were sent up from Mettapollium [Mettupalayam], in a motor car, and the vibration thereof gave them

curvature of the spine, so that they all died in very early infancy.

In an essay on 'Trout Culture in the Nilgiris', published in the *Journal of the Bombay Natural History Society* in 1920, Colonel W. Molesworth and J.F. Bryant (who was at the time Collector of the Nilgiris), narrated the long and tortuous history of these efforts. They wrote:

> In 1877, Mr. Wapshare and Mr. Hubert Knox put into the Pykara (river) some carp caught in the Ouchterlony Valley in the Wynaad. In 1879, Mr. Barlow, the Commissioner, reported that the Pykara had been stocked with Mahseer. When and by whom it was stocked, he does not say. These experimental measures were disastrous from the point of view of trout-culture. The myriads of carp in the Pykara River at the present day are too shy to be of much use to the angler. Competing as they do for the food in the river, they make it difficult for other fish to eke out a precarious living. Twelve miles of fine water from the junction of the Mukerti and Krurmund to the Pykara Waterfalls were completely spoiled...
>
> In the early eighties, fryponds were made at Pykara about 12 miles from Ootacamund. A heavy flood about the year 1884 damaged the ponds and swept the whole of the fish into the Pykara River. It was unfortunate that the accident occasioned a return to Ootacamund. Unsuitable as Pykara was owing to the existence of Carp,

it was at any rate preferable to the slopes of Snowdon and Dodabetta.

In 1884, the Game Association and the Collector reported that dynamiting and the use of small mesh nets were becoming general. A notification under Madras Act 2 of 1879 was then issued prohibiting such practices in the chief reservoirs and rivers of the plateau.

The position about this time was that the Ootacamund Lake contained Tench and Carp whilst the Pykara held numerous bony Carp. Trout were conspicuous by their absence.

In 1892, the fry kept by Dr Ross [an estate owner in Doddabetta] in a reservoir at Dodabetta were almost all lost by the breaching of the dam. In 1893, the two females of the four large fish maintained at Dodabetta spawned in February, but as the males were in milt in November, the ova could not be fertilised. In this year, seven fry-ponds and a stock-pond were made at Pykara.

Forty thousand ova imported from England were put into the icehouse at Ootacamund where they froze and were destroyed. A second consignment arrived on March 4th. The high temperature of the water, however, destroyed the fry as fast as they hatched and only 83 survived. Messrs. Ross, Marsh, Wapshare and Lawson [a group of estate owners] spent considerable sums in further attempts to propagate the species. The temperature of the water militated against success. Myriads of crabs devoured the ova as soon as they were laid. Horned owls, water-snakes, which usually occur below 6,000 feet, otters, the larvae of the dragon fly, and mildew (*Saproligneusferox*), were amongst the other enemies of the fish.

In December 1893, a consignment of 20,000 Loch Leven Ova and 29,003 Rainbow Ova were received. Despite rain and a sudden rise in temperature, almost all the rainbow trout hatched out, whilst only 572 of the brown trout fry were saved. For a time, 20 to 50 fry died daily owing to a rise in the temperature but eventually 50 were saved. However, little permanent good resulted.

Consignments of ova, mostly of *S. fario*, continued to arrive at irregular intervals. In 1900, the position was summarised by Maj. Bagnall in his article in *The Sportsman's Book For India*:

> The only trout I have seen during the year were caught during our netting operations in Snowdon ponds. Three were secured, unwholesome looking fish of about 2 lbs. each. I have heard of fish being caught in Burnfoot lake and have seen the bones of one killed by an otter.
>
> The Pykara stock pond which should have contained 19 large trout was emptied after great labour. It contained no trout, but one small fish of the Mahseer species. The caretaker, beyond remarking that he was a poor man, had no information to offer.
>
> Emerald Valley River, Avalanche and Khundah Rivers: – I have frequently hunted all along these rivers, and have seen three large trout in the Emerald Valley

River, but no sign of fish life elsewhere. Nowhere have I seen a fish as large as a little finger, and I cannot find any watcher who has.

Pykara River: – I heard a friend say he rose a trout in the Pykara River, and I hope he was not mistaken, but those who have fished there will remember how red the Mahseer look in the water.

Our present position seems to be that we know of the existence of trout in the Emerald Valley River only, and in Snowdon Ponds, in the Dodabetta Reservoirs, and in Burnfoot Lake. They probably exist also in the Marlimund Reservoir.

Fortunately, those who were putting in all this effort were also learning from their mistakes. In 1904, it was decided to import 20,000 ova of rainbow trout. The experiment in Ceylon had revealed that rainbow trout could withstand somewhat higher temperatures than the brown variety. Some 875 healthy fry raised from these ova were placed in the Parsons Valley stream. The selection of this stream was deliberate and very crucial. It contained an abundant food supply and the high falls just below the Krurmand crossing prevented the carp from the Pykara, lower down, from swimming upriver to interfere with the trout.

Two years later, when these waters were searched, a rainbow trout 14 inches long was caught. Here then was clear confirmation of the fact that trout could be established in the Nilgiris.

The government responded by beginning to pay serious attention to the fisheries sector. In July 1906, Sir F.A. Nicholson, a senior civil servant, was deputed to investigate the potential of the fishing industry in Madras Presidency. Nicholson took to the task in earnest, visiting a number of fisheries in India. His recommendation that a fisheries bureau be established in Madras was accepted in April 1907. He was first appointed honorary advisor for fisheries to the government and, three months later, was designated honorary director. Nicholson continued in the post for the next 11 years, overseeing trout acclimatization in the Nilgiris hills during his tenure.

Before these events, though, in 1906, the Nilgiri Game Association had urged Sir Arthur Lawley, governor of Madras, to obtain the services of a trained pisciculturist, perhaps from Ceylon, to develop trout culture in the Nilgiris. Lawley had written to the governor of Ceylon, who permitted an expert of the Ceylon Fishing Association to go to India. In the autumn of 1906 this expert, H.C. Wilson, arrived in Ooty.

Trout in the Nilgiris had in fact been established, at least partially, even before this expert arrived. But Wilson approached the matter systematically to fully understand where all the enthusiastic amateurs had gone wrong. He visited a number of streams, netted many stretches, and even caught a few trout. He studied the streams thoroughly, noting down everything from the temperature of the water at different times of the day, to the food available for fish and aquatic fauna, along with the local flora, etc. He even prepared two lists of streams, one where he felt trout could be established, and the other where they should not be.

Wilson's meticulousness is evident in this excerpt from the Madras Fisheries Bulletin:

> Report on Sandy Nalla stream, dated 16th November 1906.
>
> Temperature at junction of Municipal stream, at 9-30 a.m., cloudy, 58° Fahr. Temperature at noon (opposite Toda Mund), 60° Fahr. at 1-30 p.m. highest reach in shade of jungle, 58° Fahr.
>
> Remarks. – On the higher reaches after the stream divides into three runners, there is on the main source an Irish bridge, which might prevent big fish descending from the spawning ground after the flood water had subsided below the level of stones. An opening could be made to allow the passage of fish. This is a small stream and not very suitable for trout as in the dry season the upper waters will be very shallow. If trout were introduced they would descend to the Municipal stream in dry weather.
>
> The tributaries in the upper reaches are abundantly stocked with the larvas of numerous flies, especially the Notton stream. This small stream would be most suitable as a spawning ground for trout, the temperature, the nature of the bottom and natural shade in places are all that can be desired. The only fish I could see in the

> Billithada Halla were of the stone loach variety and indigenous minnow.
>
> I consider this ought to make an ideal trout river and is the best I have inspected so far. Its high elevation, low temperature, good tributaries and the fact that it is out of reach of any likelihood of poaching are all in its favour. It is capable of carrying a large number of trout and their growth should be rapid owing to the quantity of feeding.

Through his field studies, Wilson arrived at a clear understanding of what to do and where to start. Instead of using the hatching house at Ooty's Government Garden, built by Francis Day, he decided to build a more modern hatchery on a small tributary of the Avalanche stream, around 16 miles south-west of Ooty. This was an important decision. This place was a little warmer but more equable, since good shade prevented marked diurnal variations of temperature. Ooty was a little colder on the whole, but a sudden rise in temperature was not uncommon there. Besides, the water in the new place was relatively purer, while abundant vegetation ensured plentiful supplies of food.

Wilson was the first to establish that it was useless to import the ova of brown trout into the Nilgiris. The problem, he found, was that female spawned at one time and the male milted at another, so that successful and sustained reproduction was near impossible.

In 1907, Wilson went to Ceylon and returned with one hundred yearlings from the hatcheries there. These travelled safely as far as Erode, but there the train bringing the fresh supply of ice was late and the yearlings suffered severely. Only 27 survived the journey up into the hills and were finally placed in the Parsons Valley stream. Later the same year, when these waters were searched, one fish was caught on a fly, having increased four ounces in weight. This stream was then closed for fishing.

Wilson then waited for the first lot of 10,000 ova from Osnabrück in Germany, but these arrived in poor condition. The expert had to wait for the next season. Meanwhile, he prepared a report on the measures necessary to check the indiscriminate slaughter of fish in the upper waters of the large rivers of the district. He found that the native poachers on the Bhavani were rapidly emptying the river of all its fish. He was deeply concerned about the use of dynamite and other unethical methods in fishing. Based on a report by Wilson, a set of rules and regulations were notified under the Indian Fishery Act for the protection of rivers. A fishery inspector and 18 watchers were appointed. Wilson also recommended the annual propagation of the locally popular fish hilsa, which was also accepted.

In the next season, Wilson endeavoured to arrange for a fresh supply of ova from Lord Denbligh's hatcheries in Wales. However, this plan fell through owing to an unusually cold spring. Next year, in 1909, Wilson obtained 5,00,000 ova of rainbow trout from the Auckland Acclimatization Society in New Zealand. These ova reached Colombo by mail steamer in

September and were then safely bought to Avalanche in the Nilgiris. Most of these ova were successfully hatched out during the cold weather. Meanwhile, a stock pond and spawning race (a long artificial stream channel to deposit eggs) were being constructed below the hatchery. The fry were allowed to escape into the hatchery stream through the race.

The following year, 39,625 trout fry were distributed among the Avalanche, Emerald Valley, Pykara, Krurmund, Billithadhalla and Parsons Valley streams, as well as the Tiger Hill reservoir and Lovedale Lake. When thefry started to grow freely, the news was welcomed heartily by the British community of south India.

This success was noted and praised in official documents, including the *Madras Fisheries Department Bulletin* No. 12, where it was stated: 'The introduction of New Zealand trout to Nilgiri waters was successfully accomplished by Mr. Wilson in November of the previous year, but the growth during the year under report was so considerable and successful that fishing is to begin in the current year 1911. Mr. Wilson reports extraordinary trout growth, e.g., a 15 months old trout (S. irideus) 15 inches long and 8 inches round the broadest part; it was also sexually mature; many others were of nearly similar size. In November 1910, moreover, Mr. Wilson introduced ova of wild brown trout (Salmo fario) at his own charge from his hatchery in England, and these were successfully hatched and planted out; these trout operations however will be reported on by the Collector of the Nilgris.'

After this long-awaited success, some streams in the Nilgiris were thrown open for trout fishing in September 1911. The first season was inaugurated by the Madras governor Sir Arthur Lawley at Hodgson's Hut on the Krurmund stream. He caught the first trout in the adjacent pool. The season was a short one, lasting only until the end of the month. During this period 82 rods killed 137 fish, weighing 200 lb in all. The heaviest fish killed weighed 5 lb. Trout had been authoritatively established in the southern hills. As a correspondent of the *Madras Mail* wrote about the Nilgiris:

> To the keen trout angler this district is a constant source of pleasure. It is now possible to make a good basket of trout almost throughout the year. In former years trout fishing was forbidden between [the] end of September and the beginning of June. Recently certain waters have been declared open to the anglers throughout the year. Another concession is that in these waters the angler may use minnow, worm, etc. As a matter of fact the streams now open all through the year provide as good, if not better sport than those that are closed from October to June.

Sadly, the two pioneering enthusiasts of Nilgiri trout did not live to celebrate this success. For Sir William Thomas Denison had passed away in 1871 and Francis Day in 1889.

By the end of the second decade of the twentieth century, trout fishing in the Nilgiris had become a popular recreation. However, the finances of the operation were not robust. In 1912, the total revenue from licence fees was just Rs 1,495, increasing to Rs 3,400 in 1918 but then decreasing to Rs 3,096 (including Rs 306 for a mahseer licence and compounding fees). So the annual income from trout fishing was less than Rs 3,000, whereas the expenditure was around Rs 7,000. Meanwhile, the staff of the fisheries department was also demanding an increase in salary, and nobody was accounting for the depreciation of the hatchery and ponds.

The Ceylon expert, H.C. Wilson, was also not entirely satisfied with the progress of the project. He was closely monitoring the size of these fish, and by 1913 had concluded that they were smaller than anticipated. He attributed this to the lack of food in the Nilgiri streams. Wilson knew that increasing the food supply was neither easy nor immediately possible, so he tried decreasing the demand instead. He started netting to reduce the number of trout as well as reduced the size limit of fish caught, from 12 inches to 8 inches. All these efforts were to no avail (in subsequent years, the size limit was abolished).

There were also attempts to improve the food supply, by growing flowering plants and by planting watercress. Water weeds were also advocated, but trout were not growing in the Sandy Nullah Stream and Ootacamund Lake where weeds abounded. Moreover, in some places, like the Big Bend of the Mukhurti river, there was no complaint about the quality of the fishes killed. Wilson also attempted to acclimatize shrimp from the plains, as feed for trout.

When trout were placed in a pond with unlimited number of shrimp, they attained extraordinary sizes in two years. But in open waters the experiment was a failure.

In 1917, even as these experiments were being tried, H.C. Wilson, the man who had finally and firmly established the rainbow trout both in Ceylon and India, passed away. The Wilson Memorial, still standing near Pykara, reminds us of his achievements. But with his passing, the local enthusiast in the Nilgiris had to solve the problem of small fish size without the benefit of his expertise and commitment.

Meanwhile, the problem was becoming bigger. The record fish caught in 1919 was only 2 lb 25 oz, whereas in 1920 it was 2 lb 14 oz. Trout in the Nilgiris were multiplying rapidly. In their paper 'Trout Culture in Nilgiris' published in *The Journal of the Bombay Natural History Society* in 1921, Col. Molesworth and J.F. Bryant noted,

> In 1918, fishing hard for a whole week from Avalanche Bungalow and in absence of any size limit, retaining all the fish caught, the return of one of the writers (Mr. Bryant) showed a catch of 17 fish. In 1920, fishing for a week in his spare time, he caught no less than 75 fish. There was no appreciable difference in the method. More or less the same flies were used. ...The upper reaches were simply boiling with yearlings, and even in the lower stretches at Parry's Bung[a]llow and McIvor's Bund, where prior to 1920 there were few or no trout, relatively large catches might be made. The opinion

is not that of the writer alone – it is concurred in by Mr. N. E. A. Mainwaring and Col. Molesworth, IMS. Both gentlemen have in fact stated in writing that the river is overstocked.

Molesworth and Bryant also reported on some other tendencies peculiar to Nilgiri trout. These trout, they found, were 'living principally on crabs which abound at the bottom of the streams. The Nilgiri Trout after a few years becomes a bottom feeder pure and simple. He takes fly more and more shyly as the years roll by and finally ceases to rise at all.'

There was yet another problem. In 1920, almost all the trout of Yemmakal migrated, possibly into the Pykara. It was also said that after eating up all the available food, they were impelled to migrate further into the region of snakes and otters.

Other anglers thought that, rather than food supply, the reason behind the diminution in size was that new blood was required. To test this theory further, 7,500 ova of rainbow trout were imported from Kashmir in the spring of 1920, in exchange for a similar number of local ova. Most of these ova could not bear the heat of such a long journey. And by the year end, only 300 Kashmir fry were available to rear in pond No. 3 of the Avalanche hatchery. Experiments were conducted with other species of fish like the lake trout, Japanese albino trout, tiger trout and land-locked salmon, but these efforts mostly failed too.

Nonetheless, these various experiments and the introduction of new blood gave a distinct identity to Nilgiri trout. Thus, as the noted environmentalist E.R.C. Davidar remarks in the *NWA Centenary* – published in *Whispers from the Wild* by E.R.C. Davidar, 2012 –

> The Nilgiri trout is a beautiful fish iridescent with the colours of the rainbow, hence the name. Descended from many strains, including the steelhead, it has its own distinct identity. As a sporting fish it exhibits splendid fighting qualities which are best appreciated on a light fly rod. As a table fish it has few equals.

VII

TROUT IN KULLU

KULLU, THE BROAD VALLEY FORMED BY THE BEAS RIVER, rivals Kashmir for beauty and biodiversity. But, back in the nineteenth century, it could not compete in popularity among game-seekers, nor among settlers, nor even among tourists. Before the Treaty of Lahore, in 1846, Kulluwas quite hidden from the outside world. After this treaty, through which the East India Company wrested possession of Kullu from the Sikhs, along with other parts of the Punjab hills, the number of European visitors started to increase. A few came with the intention of settling permanently. The numbers increased after 1857, when India formally became a part of the British Empire. Nonetheless, the Kullu valley remained less frequented than the other hill stations of the princely state of Punjab, such as Shimla, Dalhousie, Kasauli, Palampur, Murree and Abbotabad. Located at an inconvenient distance from both Delhi and Lahore, it offered no strategic importance and there were no notable attempts to develop it.

Still, quiet and charming Kullu continued to attract those small numbers of Europeans who wanted to live peacefully, often in retirement, in the lap of nature. The prospect of hunting in the region was another attraction. Within a few years, a small European community was formed in this valley of the Beas River.

These officers and settlers tried to change the face of this lush green valley, quite as vigorously as they had done with the other hill stations. First they planted apple and other fruit. Tea was next. In 1862, a company called the Kooloo Valley Tea Company was established. Its products even won the 'Best Black Tea' of India award at an exhibition in Lahore. But the enterprise did not make much progress since the agro-climatic conditions in Kullu were not particularly favourable for tea plantation.

But this majestic V-shaped valley, spread between Manali and Largi, surrounded by massive snow-clad mountains and thick pinewood forest with a number of glacial streams, offered just as congenial conditions for trout as the Kashmir valley. After trout was acclimatized in Kashmir, Kullu was identified as the next obvious location for trout lovers in India. Kullu's European settlers were very keen on the idea, since they found no fish that afforded good sport in the river Beas. The hunter Mrs. R.H. Tyacke, wife of the Kullu settler and shikari Lt. Col. Richard Humphrey Tyacke, wrote in her book *How I Shot My Bears* published in 1893, 'Unfortunately the water of the Beas, in its passage through Kullu, is so cold that there is not a decent fish to be found in it.' The only fish found in large numbers in the river Beas was the mountain barbel (*Oreinussinuatus*), a bony fish which could was never going to appeal to European tastebuds.

Sir Louis Dane was Resident in Kashmir when trout was being acclimatized there. The experiment was close to the heart of this Sussex-born officer, and he was among those who persuaded the Kashmir government to invest in it. At the beginning of his career in India, Dane was assistant commissioner of Kangra and Kullu, so he knew very well that similar success could be achieved there too. He got a chance to test this speculation when, in 1908, he was appointed governor of Punjab.

In his very first year in office, Dane directed the assistant commissioner of Kullu, a man named Gerard Charles Lisle Howell, to go ahead with the trout experiment. Howell, unlike most other ICS men of that era, was born in India, on 16 March 1875, at Dhera Ghazi Khan (now in Pakistan), where his father Lt. Col. Horace Howell of the Bengal Staff Corps was posted at the time. G.C.L. Howell was a very popular officer in Kullu, having done much for the restoration of the region's temples, and also helping write a history of the valley. His paper 'Some Notes on Ancient Kulu Politics', published in volume 5 of the *Journal of the Panjab History Society* in 1918, is still quoted in academic circles. Howell now entered into the trout experiment with great interest, though at the time he could not have anticipated that he was embarking on a new career altogether.

Howell began with a detailed study of the Beas river and its major tributary streams, noting the temperature of the water and its condition in different stretches. Reporting his findings in the *Journal of the Bombay Natural History Society* published in 1917, he wrote:

> The true source of the Beas is in the glacial lake known as Beas Kund at the head of the Solang Valley fed from mighty glaciers which hang on the sides of an amphitheatre of peaks running up to 20,000 feet in altitude and formed by the junction of the Bara Bagahal and Mid Himalayan ranges. For the first 13 miles of its course the summer temperature of the water never rises above 46° F. Below this the temperature rises to a maximum of 56° F. at Sultanpur which is only 4,000 feet above sea level, and knows air temperatures of close on 100° F. The sward of the banks is well timbered with alder: much of the course is in summer pure cascade: but at intervals the bed widens, or is divided up by islands into what might be called (by comparison) 'flats.' Still men who essay to fish the Beas must be men who have learnt, or are willing to learn, the art of fishing 'white water' if they would make big baskets. With some of the tributaries it is different. The lower two miles of the Beas Rikki, for instance, the Sarbarri, the Upper Sainj, and the Tirthan and the Bathad Brook are comparatively quiet waters on which any man who understands Irish or Welsh or Scotch mountain streams should be able to kill fish.

Howell studied the entire fauna of the Beas Valley, exploring both the availability of food for trout and the possible effect of the introduction of trout on the local fauna. He even tried to identify potential enemies of the fish. These included otters and kingfishers, as well as local poachers. Of this last category he wrote:

> Homo sapiens in the Inner Hills has not yet developed much ingenuity in the gentle art of destroying fish simply because he has no knowledge of species sufficiently toothsome to inspire him. At present he 'fishes fair' for the most part with a casting net. A heavy spate drives trout to the banks to seek for the surface food washed in by the rain, and at such times they can be taken easily enough with a casting net. But unless the water is well coloured experiment shows that trout are much too quick for the most skilful netsman, and they generally lie in heavy water where a net must carry away. There will be little difficulty in preventing netting in the reaches reserved for anglers. That fish poaching will sooner or later attract Kulu men – once they have acquired a taste for trout – goes without saying. But that time is not yet. The main danger will be poisoning and diversion of the Nursery streams.

Having done his homework thoroughly, Howell now awaited the arrival of ova from Kashmir. In February 1909, a batch of 30,000 trout ova was sent down to Kullu, under the supervision of Sohdama, the Kashmiri assistant of Frank James Mitchell, who by this time had become a hatching expert. Accompanying him was a hatchery keeper from Kullu who had apprenticed with Sohdama. When this batch of ova reached Kullu safely, it is said that Mr. Howell was so happy that he gifted his pocket watch to Sohdama (though there is no mention of this reward in any of the records of that time). What is on record, though, is that in 1915, when the biggest trout caught thus far in Kashmir was recorded, Frank Mitchell sent a photograph of this fish with Sohdama wearing the watch around his neck to the *Journal of the Bombay Natural History Society*. In a note accompanying the photo, Mitchell wrote, 'I sent him with the first ova to Kulu, where at the time Mr. Howell was Assistant Commissioner, and the watch he is wearing in the photo was presented to him by the Punjab Government in recognition of his services there.'

Assisting Howell in his work was General Osborn, a fisherman and naturalist who had settled in the Kullu valley. The general had a beautiful villa near the Tripura Sundari temple, close to the stream where the trout experiment was to be conducted. As the Lahore newspaper, *Civil and Military Gazette* in its 22nd February 1910 edition wrote, 'Mr. Howell entered on the experiment with the greatest interest, and recorded all the various phases of the trial with most minute care.' Howell conducted two experiments simultaneously: stocking the streams directly and creating a breeding nursery. He made a hatching house near Naggar, with a nursery pond, and put in 10,000 ova there. He placed the rest of the ova directly into the various tributaries ofthe Beas – 9,000 in the Saran stream, 6,000 in Harripur, 2,000 in Naih Behal and 3,000 in Chakki. These ova were not literally poured into the stream but were kept in the 'pahari' boxes developed by Frank Mitchell in Kashmir, not more than 2,000 ova to a box, between layers of moss. These boxes were then covered with a lid to keep out the light. Arrangements were made to inspect these ova daily. As it turned out, almost all hatched out well with 47 days, with no more casualties than might be expected. In due course, the fry liberated themselves through the holes at the top of the boxes and swam away upstream. Now they were on their own.

Trout, when it first emerges from the egg, has a little transparent umbilical sac. This sac contains all the food that tiny fish need. But when the sac is gradually absorbed they begin to seek their food elsewhere. It was found that the young fish used the boxes as a nest for a while, returning to them for safety after their expedition for food. But within a few weeks this stage too ended and the boxes emptied. It was also reported that frogs and other predatory animals had taken their toll.

As Howell later wrote about this technique:

> The great advantage of this method is that fish are from the first dawn of consciousness 'wild' fish feeding on natural food. It eliminates the human element and all danger of mistakes in feeding. It is a sine qua non that the water chosen should abound in Natural Food,

> which roughly speaking will be the case wherever water cress and other water plants grow: the spring should not exceed 55° [F] in temperature, and its maximum summer temperature should not exceed 63° F. It is necessary to employ a man to 'pick over' the eggs in all boxes distant from the Hatchery, i.e., to remove all 'dead' eggs and alevins. This method succeeds best in spring water with a constant temperature. Snow water varies immensely in temperature and is subject to spates especially in March, and these variations kill alevins in large quantities.

Meanwhile, the ova placed in the Naggar trout pond were doing well but facing their own sets of problems. According to a picturesque report in the *Civil and Military Gazette,*

> The ten thousand ova were all hatched out by the beginning of the May and began to feed, their diet being on the first day fresh Bardel, on the second, liver and on the third dried prawn from Bombay, in regular rotation. Before this some 2,000 alevins had been removed from the pond on account of deformities of sorts, so that 8,000 alevins were left in the nursery pond till July 1st when stock was taken. It was then found that the differences in the size of fishes were almost incredible, and seventeen very large fishes, who were undoubtedly cannibals, were removed and let loose in the stream, while over two thousand were placed in the

stock pond. In the middle of October another stock taking was held. Again the same difference in size was discovered, twenty-eight fish being much too big, and it's believed that these big fish and the seventeen other criminals which were exiled in July, had accounted for over 4,000 young fish. At the close of the season it was found that, excluding the 2,000 crippled in the egg stage, 2,274 yearlings had been reared from 8,000 ova, or an average of 33 percent, which compare well with the best results obtained in trout farms in England. In the nursery pond fifty two large fish were kept apart. They were distinctly bad dispositioned fish, sulky, lurking, bottom feeding brutes, but efforts were being made to educate them into better manners by keeping them out of the way of temptation in a very heavy stream.

Later, it was decided to keep as many trout in the pond as might be required for breeding, and to distribute those not required among other streams in the Kullu valley. According to an article by Howell, in 1909 a total of 22,862 trouts were released into the different waters of the Valley. He also wrote that the maximum number of young trout (approximately 19,000) were released into the five miles of fishable water between Kelat and Katrain.

In the summer of 1910, when a dozen trout were caught at Katrain, ranging from 8 to 11 inches long, it was quite clear that the experiment had been extremely successful. The following year a trout that weighed over

3 lbs and was 20 inches long was found in the same place. Of these developments Howell remarked: 'These fish weigh about 25 percent more than the average English fish of the same length. This is due no doubt to the plentiful feed in the Beas, and to the torrential character of much of its course, which secures oxygenisation at all points.'

Howell continued to stock the different streams of the valley. From 1913, he stocked these streams in large numbers by using ova imported from Kashmir – 9,600 in 1913, 41,253 in 1914, 51,406 in 1915. In 1914, he even stocked the Uhl river, outside the Kullu valley.

While his hatchery was working overtime and the stocking operation was in full swing, Howell found that trout were also breeding in rivers. As he later wrote:

> It is a little hard of course as a rule to say that a particular trout caught anywhere in the river is or is not one of the fish bred in and released from the Hatchery. But in June 1914 and again in June 1915 large number of trout fry about 2 inches long, considerably longer than their domesticated contemporaries who average only one inch, were caught and examined in the Katrain Brook Nursery. ...This brook was stocked with 2000 eyed ova in 1909; and has been left to its own resources ever since. ...It is fed both by spring and by snow water and is in every way an ideal little trout stream running through older copses with deep holes, overchanging banks, and water-cress beds at frequent intervals. It is particularly certain that neither in 1914 nor in 1915 have any fry

planted by us found their way into this brook; nor would domesticated fry have attained an average length of two inches by June.

Though the trout were breeding naturally in the Kullu Valley, Howell wanted to breed them artificially too. His opinion was that 'in Nature – which has not allowed for the destruction by mankind – very few fish survive through the egg stage and the larval stage to adult trouthood. The egg have of course no means of defence; the larvae or alvins can move indeed but cannot steer a course or make any connected effort to avoid a pursuer; and in a tragic world which lies beneath the surface of the water there is no thought of mercy for any living thing which can neither fight nor flee. ...Fishiculture, in one sentence, eliminates that danger period altogether.' He went on to note that '49 breeding fish gave us over gave them over 40,000 fish in 1914,' and that if they had left them to their own devices, he doubted that more than 400–500 would have made it. As he put it,'It is merely a case of supplementing Nature's methods.'

While Howell was busy stocking the streams of Kullu, World War I had broken out. Far from enjoying angling in these streams, British soldiers became engaged in a fight for country and empire. Howell wrote in the *Journal of the Bombay Natural History Society*: 'I hope that the fish are in the Beas awaiting the return of the natural times when soldier men may have time to fish for them, and that all the natural conditions are in favour of stock increasing.'

Howell's hope was not misplaced. But even before the war ended, the region had begun to draw enthusiastic anglers. Among them was J.G. Brooker, who went in 1917, and wrote as quoted in *The Mighty Mahseer and Other Fish*:

> I fished from May 1st to June 5th. I got 50 trout, average size just under 1 lb. Several were 2 lbs. and over, the best I got was 22 inches in length though he only scaled 4 lbs. I also got 400 Barbels, average weight 1 lb. The largest Barbel was about 4 lbs. and I got many of 3 lbs. There are no trout below Sultanpur. Commencing at Sultanpur I got a few fish of 3/4 lb. but nothing much bigger. Seven or eight miles further up, near Aramgarh and Raisan there are some nice pools. Then a couple of miles further on at Dobi the fishing is excellent, and from Dobi to Katrain very good. From Sultanpur to Katrain is 12 miles. Above Katrain I never got a fish, though I fished to Manali 12 miles from Katrain. The main river at these places is very big, and is nothing like the ordinary trout stream, you only fish along the edges, in pools behind stones, and in bays where the water is slack. In June the snows begin to melt and the river is in flood. I understand that it remains so till the rains are over about September...

A few years later, in 1922, Brooker wrote to Cecil Lang, 'I have never revisited Kulu but I have heard from a correspondent there that fishing conditions have improved.'

Cecil Lang himself was convinced of the success of Howell's experiment. As he wrote in his book,

> The girth of the fish indicates that the Kulu breed is likely to be a fine one: and the fact that a trout has been landed at Mandi shows that trout fishing is likely to extend from the mouth of the Suketi Khad in Mandi to the source of the Beas. That is to say roughly from the point where Mahseer fishing stops, and above which only the insipid mountain barbel (*Oreinussinuatus*) is caught. There is no reason in fact why the Naggar hatchery should not fill over 150 miles of water, at present practically useless as a fishery, with one of the most valuable of fresh-water species.

Howell had calculated the length of the trout water in the main Beas River as being around 116 miles, running from the point where the Solang river met the Beas to the point where the Tirthan met it. He divided the whole into ten reaches of fishable water in a map, with a comment that 'strange names are always rather a nuisance, so in the Map I have numbered the "reaches" of trout water so far stocked'. He studied the entire area so thoroughly that the names were no longer 'strange', at least to him, as his writing reveals: 'Between Sultanpur and Larji the river will be netted, and trout fishing is never likely to be good. It is never safe to attempt to ford the Beas. It is bridged only at Larji, Bhuin, Sultanpur, Raisan, Katrain, Kelat and Manali. Above this temporary bridges cross it at

Palchan, Solang, and in summer at Dhundi. This means that a man will, as a rule, be able to fish one bank only on the same day, unless he is camped near a bridge.'

During the course of his experiment Howell noticed that trout even found their way further to Mandi, below the point where mahseer fishing starts.

Howell advised anglers that for a stretch of 41 miles, from Manali to Akhara Bridge, they should carry 30 rods, as the river was so broad and the flow of water so torrential that no one would be able to fish both banks on the same day. In 1914, he estimated that there were at least 500,000 trout in the first seven reaches, including the fish naturally spawned in the river.

The experiment in Kullu was a grand success. Soon a department of fisheries was formed in Punjab, with its headquarters at Lyallpur, known as the first planned city of British India (now in Pakistan and renamed Faisalabad). Howell was made the founding director of this department. He became so deeply involved in fish and fisheries, that after his retirement,he settled in Canada and wrote his famous *Ocean Research and the Great Fisheries* published in 1921, which still holds its place in the canon of ichthyology.

In 1915, when Howell left Kullu, C.H. Donald was appointed the warden of fisheries. Donald was an environmentalist and a Fellow of the Zoological Society of London. Before this posting he worked as a forest officer in various Himalayan districts. Donald was also a resident of the valley, owning a property near Dobi, a village on the banks of the Beas. In 1912, while trying to solve the problem of transportation of huge logs of wood from the hills to the plains below, Donald developed a system of aerial ropeways based on traction by gravity. This system, called Donald's gravity ropeway, became widely used in the Himalaya for the extraction of scantlings from inaccessible areas. It could be used on slopes ranging from 17 to 45 degrees.

Donald's principal interest was in birds. He wrote a number of papers on bird life and bird behaviour for the *Journal of the Bombay Natural History Society*. However, after taking charge of fisheries in Kullu, he gave a professional touch to operations in this sphere. By this time the Punjab Fisheries Act of 1914 had come into existence. Donald first tried to strengthen the infrastructure of trout breeding. In addition to the hatchery at Chakki Nala, he developed a full-fledged stock pond nursery at Mahili, across the river from Katrain, where, apart from the usual breeding ponds, there was a hospital tank to house sick fish, as well as sorting tanks for striped fish.

Lt. Col. Richard Humphrey Tyacke, in his book *Fish and Fishing in Kulu* written in 1941, provides rich details of the hatchery and stock pond:

> At the hatchery in Chakki Nala are one hatchery shed and four rearing ponds, holding breeding stock of different ages from one to three years. On approaching their third year they are taken down to the stock pond, where they are stripped, as at this age they are usually fit for spawning. The rule is that the number of cock

and hen fish in the stock pond should be approximately equal, though if the cocks slightly exceeds the hens it does not matter. There were in 1917, 80 females and 74 cocks in the ponds, and more cocks were required to be caught to make up the deficiency.

Tyacke also tells us that the native barbel fish of the Beas, which never appealed to Europeans, soon became the favourite of the trouts at the stock pond. They were fed with the finely chopped barbel, and 'a little common salt, which act[s] as a tonic'. About the ageing fish in the stock pond he further wrote, 'In the stock ponds, fish over six years are consider[ed] as too old for breeding, and these are sold to anyone who wishes to buy them, the present rate being eight anna[s] a pound, but they cannot be recommended for the table as they are generally woolly and tough.'

Soon, a Fisheries Research Laboratory was also established in Kullu, with a research officer appointed to analyse the fish food and its quantity available in different streams, study local insect fauna and keep an eye on fish diseases.

These efforts resulted in a good number of trout in the Beas and its tributaries. And when the war ended, British officers and other Europeans started to pour into the valley for trout angling. In 1923 only 17 fishing licences were issued, by 1930 this number had increased to 90, and a decade later it was over 300. While Kashmir had established itself as the prime angling destination in north India, Kullu was not far behind.

A Kullu settler, T. Tyson, even wrote a guidebook in 1934 for visitors: *Trout Fishing in Kulu*. The book's blurb helpfully informed readers that it contained 'a brief description of the rivers, routes and accommodations available for visitors'. Written originally for those who knew nothing about Kullu, this book become so popular that within seven years a second edition was published.

In this book, apart from offering information on the trout fishing to be had in the Beas River, Tyson spoke of the joy of fishing in its tributaries. On the other hand, Tyacke, in his book, was doubtful about the prospects of fishing in these lesser streams, which, he wrote, were 'generally too rapid for fishing'. Tyacke continued: 'If the fish in the Sainj and Tirthan have not been extensively poached, these two rivers would probably be very favourable, but it is impossible to say what is, or has been, going on there, for no European lives near them, and I do not think that many licensed anglers have fished the waters, so that if there are any fish there, they would be at least unsophisticated.'

In the preface to the first edition of his guidebook, Tyson acknowledged that in Kullu, 'the sport is not so well organized and protected as in Kashmir – nor is it so expensive. Social amenities and modern conveniences are particularly non existent and apart from dak bungalows and official rest houses, accommodation is extremely limited.' But, he added, 'In spite of these disadvantages Kulu possesses an almost irresistible charm for those who have experienced its tranquil environment and, year after year, a few familiar faces may be seen. The valley has a charm of its own which cannot easily be matched in other parts of the Himalayas; it still retains its atmosphere of unruffled peace and its loveliness is as yet unspoilt by commercial exploitation.'

However, the second edition of the book spoke of the deteriorating condition of trout in the Beas. In the preface to this edition, Tyson remarked:

> During the intervening years there have been changes, but none sufficiently drastic to disturb the leisurely charm of this beautiful valley. As a holiday resort Kullu is becoming more popular and the number of visitors is increasing, year by year. To meet the growing demand further accommodation has had to be provided at main residential centres, while additional amenities like tennis, golf and swimming have gradually come into existence, though not yet on a scale comparable with the other Himalayan playgrounds. ...Trout fishing on some of the rivers has, in recent years, deteriorated to a certain extent, but still remains the principal attraction. The Fisheries Department is striving hard to eradicate the cause of this deterioration and to restore all rivers and streams to their condition when fishing was at its best. Rules and license fees have undergone alteration, but general conditions vary little from those originally prescribed and despite the slight increase in the licence fees, trout fishing in this valley is still an alluring and inexpensive sport.

While Tyson did not go into the reasons for this deterioration, Tyacke offered a number of explanations. Thus he wrote, 'The river is far from being really suitable for trout, from the breeding point of view at all events; the gravel bed[s] are hard to find and with the constant floods to which the Beas is subject, must be frequently washed away and so much spawn destroyed.' On another page he says, 'It must be remembered, however, that the Beas in Kullu is not by any means an ideal trout river...' A large section of his book was devoted to 'Enemies of Trout', where he concluded that, apart from other hostile elements, native poachers were the biggest threat for trout in the Beas. As in his previous book, *The Sportsman's Manual* published in 1907, here too he betrayed his antipathy towards the local population. Thus, Tyacke wrote:

> Another trouble, and one difficult to contend with, is poaching! To watch a river for a length of 100 miles, when there is no European Inspector, and when, during the poaching season which is principally during the winter months, there are seldom more than half a dozen Europeans living in the valley, is an impossibility. For three or four months in the year when the snow-fields are solid, the river is so low that the fish congregate in pools, and are therefore an easy prey for the poachers, who doubtless take full advantage, and the fish poison can also be resorted to. With little or no fear of detection, could the Kulu man resist such a chance of getting something for nothing? I doubt it.

This animus against poachers in Kullu is inexplicable, since there were no ready markets for trout nearby, nor were there all-weather roads and the infrastructure to send fish to distant markets. The perishable trout fish could not have borne a journey of more than a week. Impoverished peasants were fishing only for subsistence, but this too the territorial colonials could not brook.

Trout in Kullumay have been facing many problems – poaching (such as it was), predatory otters, kingfishers and mahseer, and then the floods. Nonetheless, it was beyond any doubt that the aquatic beauty of European streams had been established in the valley of the gods. Anglers from all over India started to pour into Kullu for long holidays. This started to put pressure on tourist infrastructure in the valley. Tyson devoted two full chapters of his book to the availability of accommodation (or lack thereof) and other facilities. He wrote, 'The insistent demand for accommodation in Kulu, beyond that available in dak bungalows and departmental rest-houses, has gradually broken down the conservative insularity which originally existed in this out-of-the-way valley.'

VIII

TROUT IN TRAVANCORE

FAVOURABLE CLIMATIC CONDITIONS AND THE DOGGED efforts of G.C.L. Howell combined effectively to establish trout in the streams of Kullu in the first attempt. But in hill stations elsewhere in India, success was more elusive. As for example in the hills of the princely state of Travancore, known as the 'Kashmir of the South'.

Through the eighteenth century, these hills were out of reach for the British, because the ruler of Mysore, Tipu Sultan, kept them at bay. Three decades after Tipu's death, Benjamin Swain Ward and Peter Eyre Conner, lieutenants of the Madras Infantry, did a trigonometric survey of the hills and mountain peaks of Travancore. These hills in the southernmost stretch of the Western Ghats had begun to attract European adventure-seekers. A cool climate, untouched natural beauty, and rich flora and fauna were on offer. The forest tracts of these hills afforded some of the best sport in India. In 1893, as the missionary Rev. Samuel Mateer wrote in his book *Native Life in Travancore*, '... sportsmen and the naturalist will find an endless variety in the fauna; elephants and tigers, for instance, so numerous in some parts that the hillmen are obliged to build their huts on tops of trees – wild oxen and deers, monkeys, crocodiles, snakes, birds, fishes and insects.'

In 1877, when Henry Gribble Turner of the Madras civil services, along with his half-brother A.W. Turner, also known as 'Thambi' (younger brother in Tamil) Turner, came here for a shikar expedition, they were mesmerised by the grandeur of the hills. They also realised the vast commercial potential of the terrain. H.G. Turner contacted the local chief, himself subordinate to the Maharaja of Travancore, and obtained a lease for 227 square miles of land. He sensed that these hills would be suitable for tea, cardamom, cinchona, coffee and sisal plantations. At this time there were only thick forests with a variety of wild animals; the area was completely undeveloped in a commercial sense. After purchasing the land, H.G. Turner founded the North Travancore Land Planting and Agricultural Society, whose members developed their own estates in various parts of the High Ranges. A number of small holders began to purchase plots and planted a variety of crops there. Thambi Turner was the first to start cultivation near the Devikulam lake. The first tea bush was planted by a certain A.H. Sharp at Parvathi in 1880.

John Daniel Munro was the first coffee planter in these hills. He was the son of Gen. John Munro, who after serving in the East India Company for several years became the diwan of Travancore state. The younger

Munro played a leading role in the activities of the North Travancore Land Planting and Agricultural Society. Meanwhile, a Glasgow firm named Finally Group bought 33 estates in the region. These were brought together in a company named after the Kanan Devan Hills in which they were situated.

Writing about these hills in July 1881, the London magazine *The Field*, remarked: 'The property comprises table land, from 4,500 to 6,000 ft in elevation, cut by valleys and ridges clothed with forests, interspersed with grassy glades. Each valley has its watercourse and the subject for regret is that the crystal clear streams contain no trout, for it would be impossible to suggest any more promising looking water.'

As the number of European settlers in these hills grew, a new town emerged on the map, named Munnar. In this town, the planters formed the Gymkhana Club, which later became the High Range Club. It was started with a loan of Rs 2,500 from the Kanan Devan Hills Produce Co. Ltd. This was a pioneering planters' club in many ways: the first residential club, the first to be electrified, and among the first to get a telephone connection.

It was in this club that, one cosy evening in 1909, four planters named M.C. Koechlin, John Carless, 'Daisy' Bell and George Howlett were chatting over a drink. Their discussion, almost inevitably, moved to trout. They were quite aware of what had transpired in Ceylon, the Nilgiris and Kashmir, and were hopeful that a similar experiment would succeed in the cool atmosphere of these hills. After a long debate, the quartet decided to approach Patrick Robertson Buchanan for help. Educated at the University of Glasgow, Buchanan was general manager of the Kanan Devan Hills Produce Company. He saw merit in their suggestion and decided to go ahead with the experiment, even in the absence of a pisciculturist like H.C. Wilson or an officer-turned-expert like G.C.L. Howell. This was the first trout project in India where the government was not involved directly, since it was financed by a private company.

Soon, arrangements were made to import the eyed ova of brown trout from a hatchery at Howieton in Stirlingshire. The consignment was sent to Bombay with all the necessary precautions. By the time it reached Bombay, Philip Gouldsbury, a senior officer of the James Finlay tea company, was there to receive it. The distance from Bombay to Travancore was almost a thousand miles. In 1909, it must have been challenging to transport the ova in ice-cold temperature over such a long distance by road and rail. Nonetheless, Philip Gouldsbury managed to convey the precious cargo successfully to its destination.

A detailed account of these efforts to plant trout in Travancore is contained in a contemporary essay published in the *Journal of the Bombay Natural History Society*. The author was W.S.S. Mackay, manager of the Rajamallay Estate and a major shareholder of the North Travancore Land Planting and Agricultural Society. Notably, this essay makes no mention of any difficulties faced by Philip

Gouldsbury, though other consignments are referred to. Thus Mackay wrote:

> On another occasion a box containing 10,000 ova was duly delivered by the Howieton people into the charge of M. C. Koechlin returning from leave on board a ship sailing from Liverpool. No details are available of this particular voyage or of the difficulties experienced if any, but it is known that the operation was successful. In those days transport difficulties were considerable, so when the chest of ova arrived at Colombo it had to be transhipped to a coasting vessel bound for Tuticorin. In the absence of cold storage facilities aboard the coaster large supplies of ice had to be arranged for. At Tuticorin ice was required for the train journey to Kodaikanal Road Station, and lastly for the 75 miles drive by bullock cart to the bottom of the riding ghat, where the chest was taken over and carried by headload to Top Station, an elevation 6,200' above sea level. On one such expedition, the last of its kind, which was undertaken by George Strachan in 1913, the ice ran out uncomfortably far from his destination, but with good fortune, and by hurrying on the coolies, he succeeded in reaching the High Range...

When the first consignment of ova reached, a newly constructed hatchery was awaiting it. It was constructed at Chundavurrai Estate under the supervision of its manager, John Carless. H.A. Ragg, a planter of Kanan

Devan Hills and a naturalist, was also present to help hatch out the ova.

W.S.S. Mackay gives an interesting account of the whole operation:

> This hatchery was situated about a mile from the Chundavurrai factory. It was a simple enough affair, the water being led in from an open channel broken at several points by silt traps, to a distributing trough, from which two hatching troughs were supplied. The whole construction was of timber and the final filtration of the water was accomplished by fitting in wooden frames covered with towelling at the head of the troughs. In theory the system was adequate, but in practice somewhat unsatisfactory. All day and throughout most of the night a reliable overseer, which generally turned out to be one of the European Managers of a neighbouring Estate, was compelled to be in attendance, constantly changing the filters which had become clogged with dirt, and keeping an eye on the flow of the water. History does not record all the difficulties they overcame, but it is a matter of great credit to them that they succeeded in hatching a very reasonable percentage of the ova they had imported all the way from Scotland.

We don't have details about how the hatching was accomplished. What we do know is that between 1909 and 1914 around 25,000 ova were imported, and about 10,000 fine little trout hatched out at Chundavurrai. As

Mackay recalled: 'When all the difficulties of transport in those days are considered this percentage must be looked upon as remarkable. The work was undertaken without the aid of any informative literature regarding trout culture in the East such as we have to-day, or the help of such experienced men as would be readily available at home.'

The first batch of young trout was liberated into the Kundaly and some other streams. Though partial success was recorded in some places, on the whole the experiment was not successful. According to Mackay, 'These trout made their way downstream, but alas many of them fell into the hands of poachers who set nets and night lines in the vicinity of Madupatty Estate. Some were also liberated at Kanniamallay and Guderale and J.M. Bridgmail and E.H. Francis stocked the Othaparai stream, but few of these fish were seen again. Trout were taken to the wilds of Hamilton's Plateau and were liberated in the Eruvikulam river by A.W. John and a fellow planter, and these trout did exceedingly well. As far as we know no natural breeding of Brown Trout took place in this or any other High Range water.'

Within a few years, though, news of brown trout being caught started to emerge from the hills of Travancore. It is said that Henry Gribble Turner was the first to catch trout there.

Mackay described the event vividly:

> H. G. Turner, who was a servant of the Government of Madras, was on the eve of retirement when he

experienced a desire to revisit, for the last time, the hills he loved so much. In company with an old friend, 'Toby' Martin, another pioneer of the District, who was at that time in charge of Labour Recruiting at Bangalore, he camped out in the wild country of Hamilton's Plateau, in the vicinity of Aneimudi. One evening as they sat on a ridge above the headwaters of the Eruvikulam river, on the look-out for a herd of Bison, they were astonished to see through their glasses unmistakable rings, apparently made by trout rising, in the still part of the river. They had no idea that any trout had been put into this river, and it was only then that they understood from the hillmen with them, that trout stocking operations had taken place the previous year.

The frequent and determined rises must have been altogether too much for these old warriors, for they at once proceeded to cut suitable lengths of cane from the forest with which to make a rod. The hook they fashioned from an old safety pin, and then all the lengths of string that could be collected from amongst their camp kit were joined together, a few grasshoppers were captured, and there they were ready for an experiment in dapping.

There was a high wind ruffling the water when they reached the bank, and every now and then, particularly in the vicinity of the wild Rhododendron bushes that overhang the banks, there would be the 'plop' of a considerable trout. Gathering a length of line in his hand Turner gently released the baited hook on the water, the breeze taking it down stream and gradually

> straightening out the line. Anxiously they watched the 'hopper' float past a bush. Then with a swirl and a suck the bait was drawn under the surface and he was fast into a splendid fish. Fortunately he must have been able to clear the bush and play his fish from the open bank beyond, for it was duly landed and weighed over the pound, a perfect speckled beauty of the variety known as Salmo fario, the Brown Trout. Several trout were taken in this manner and thus 'H. G.'s' last visit to these hills must have been all the more memorable for him.

When the news of brown trout in Eravikulam spread, a number of anglers started to visit the high range. However, since no records were maintained, we don't know the sizes of the fish caught. There is only one mention of a trout weighing 3 lb, probably the biggest, which was caught at Periavurrai by M.C. Koechlin.

Soon World War I broke out and the Kanan Devan Company was no longer interested in importing ova. When the stock of brown trout in local streams ran out, the whole experiment was deemed a failure. In 1932, a full 14 years after the war ended, A.W. John, a planter of Chittavurrai who had also played a lead role in stocking the Eravikulam river, started to dream about the matter afresh. He even created a number of small lakes in his estate for this purpose. He asked the company for permission, saying that he would undertake the experiment on his own accord.

John's plan was simple. Instead of importing ova from overseas, he decided to bring rainbow trout ova from a hatchery in the Nilgiris. His conviction was that if rainbow trout could succeed in the neighbouring Nilgiri hills they could succeed in the High Range too. He left Chittavurrai for the Nilgiris with A.J.E. Steven, another planter of the area and a very active naturalist. As quoted in 'Conflict with the Game', Steven wrote of their expedition:

> We set out full of high hope one early cold weather morning, but luck seemed against us; the SPMR lorry which was to bring the fish back broke down before it passed Nymakkad, but we carried on and decided to hire a lorry in Ooty. This we succeeded in doing and the next morning, having sent the hireling ahead were on our way to Avalanche when the back axle of John's car broke. We commandeered another lorry working on the road to take us the rest of the way to the hatchery, and eventually collected the trout and started back for the high range. It was an all night journey with all of us John, myself, Manuel from the hatchery, driver, cleaner, and of course the fish, all crowded into a rather rickety lorry. It was a mighty tired party which reached Chittavurrai next morning, but we got there with a very reasonable percentage of our Rainbow fry alive and kicking.

John stocked these fry in the lakes he had created on his estate at the north-east edge of the Company's concession overlooking the plains of Madura and at an elevation of 6,154 ft. According to Mackay, his plan was 'sound enough in theory, but incorrect so far as his particular conditions were concerned. He hoped that his trout might thrive, and even breed in the feeder streams leading into his lakes, but in this he was disappointed. Yearling fry, fingerlings were brought in fish carriers by lorry from the hatchery at Avalanche on several occasions. Supplies of ice were arranged at various points such as Coimbatore, Pollachi and Udamalpet, and the journey was undertaken at night. It was an arduous task demanding considerable endurance. The latter part of this journey up the narrow winding ghat road to the hills was generally undertaken as dawn began to break, and it was with relief that the cold air of the hills was felt and the back of the journey broken.'

The outcome of this experiment was described by Mackay as follows:

> Mr. John at first transported a few hundred trout successfully. For 18 months he watched these trout rising freely, and then he allowed a few friends to fish the water. At the first outing five fish weighing 10 1/2 lbs. were caught and throughout the season fish ranging from 2 to 4 lbs. were taken. The second year a fish of 5 lbs. was caught but thereafter nothing. The lakes were stocked again with similar experiences but the big fish disappeared altogether. These lakes which were in actual fact acting as large silt traps, contained, latterly, many feet of thick black mud at the bottom. That the bigger fish died, many of them spawnbound and that they buried themselves in the mud, would be a likely explanation for their disappearance. In spite of the fact

that this undertaking had been a failure, Mr. John had stimulated interest again, and our successes of to-day are very largely due to his keenness and determination.

Now the fishing scene in the High Range was suddenly reanimated. In 1934 a small angling association was formed, primarily financed by J.S.B. Wallace, general manager of the Kanan Devan Company. A further donation and subscription drive was launched to import a fresh batch from Avalanche. The association gained popularity overnight and as membership grew they decided to build a new hatchery at Aravikkad. But it did not prove successful. Again in 1937, another hatchery was built by A.J.E. Steven, but once more the experiment foundered. There were rapid ups and downs in the temperature of the water, so the importat of eyed ova from the Nilgiris failed.

Meanwhile some planters collected private funds to stock Devikulam and Loch Finlay. But again luck did not favour them. Though the fish survived, they were not found to be breeding.

Around this time, the new general manager of the Kanan Devan Company, E.H. Francis, took charge of the Angling Association. He came to the conclusion that 'no natural breeding of Rainbow trout could be expected at an elevation under 6,000 feet,' as mentioned by Mackay in his 1944 article. Artificial lakes and ponds were quite unsuitable for these fish, as the big fish disappeared within the first year or two and many of these probably died spawn-bound. It was thought probable that fish died on reaching an age of approximately 5 years, but information on this point was still being sought. The hatchery site had been unhappily chosen and must be considered a dead loss.

Some planters believed that, in the Eravikulam river at Hamilton's Plateau, trout would not only survive but also multiply. Others thought that 'beyond Hamilton's Plateau further magnificent water at Puar and Kalar was clearly indicated on the map, while at Rajamallay Estate a splendid river drains out to the west.' W.S.S. Mackay was manager of the Rajamallay Estate and he built a new hatchery at the foothills of Anamudi.

Mackay gives some details about the stocking of the Eravikulam river there:

> At the hatchery we had some two hundred fry, and a few yearling trout, which had been earmarked for Eruvikulam. In spite of some opposition, the Committee decided to move these fry during the heavy monsoon of 1937 to Hamilton's Plateau, and liberate them in the headwaters of the Eruvikulam River. At that time there were no roads across the plateau, the last Estate path ending at the edge of the Upper Vagavurrai Tea Estate, below the 'Knife Back' ridge. From Arivikad the trout were transported by lorry in earthenware pots, and from the Upper Vagavurrai Bungalow by head-load. The expedition, in the height of a heavy monsoon burst, was no mean undertaking, but the fish travelled well,

and the porters put up a very fine display of endurance. The expedition was well supplied with rum which put heart into the men for the homeward journey in the evening. Not a single fish was lost during the transport and as the temperature was steadily dropping in the carriers during the whole journey they were liberated almost at once. It was a wonderful sight to see the little chaps wriggle off so fit and well, and to feel that, at all events, the first stocking of this magnificent water had been accomplished.

This water was once more stocked in 1938 with 500 fry, brought from the Nilgiris by a hatchery attendant. But proper care was not taken en route, and only 301 could be liberated into the water, the rest perishing. During this restocking operation it was also decided to check if the trout of the previous year were still in the water. A rod was put into the water by Mackay, and he hooked quite a big trout in perfect condition in his second effort.

The same year, the mountaineer Lt. Gen. Edward Felix Norton came to the Western Ghats with his wife for a holiday. They went to the Eravikulam river with Mackay and killed a big trout, a full 20 lb in weight.

When the water of the Eravikulam proved to be a suitable breeding stream, it was decided to rearrange the whole hatchery system. At that time there were four hatcheries in the area, at Devikulam, Kanniamallay, Loch Finlay and Rajamallay. It was found that these four were inadequate to stock the river, and another hatchery was built at the Rajamallay Estate. Mackay was in charge, and he had taken care of everything, from silt to gravel and from the aeration of water to the temperature of the stream. This project was so successful that in 1943, 14,000 ova from pond and wild spawners were taken and 70 per cent were hatched out successfully.

IX

TROUT, TROUT, EVERYWHERE

ON A FINE MORNING IN THE LATE SUMMER OF 1912, G.C.L. Howell, the assistant commissioner of Kullu, received a request to send 2,000 trout ova to the beautiful but small and mostly unknown Gaj stream of Kangra. Howell was doubtful about Gaj's suitability for brown trout, so his response was discouraging. On 22 August 1912, he wrote to the secretary of the Punjab government: 'As I am by no means certain that these Kangra streams are likely to prove suitable for brown trout, I would suggest that no further expenditure be at present incurred on experiments with this species without reference to me. I will submit a note later when I have completed certain data as to water temperature in the Beas right bank tributaries,' adding, 'The result of my enquiries to date is that the rainbow trout (Salmo irideus) are likely to do better than Salmo fario in Gaj. Caution is all the more admirable that we are incurring the additional expense in perfecting the more important Kullu experiment.'

Howell's disinclination to send trout to a remote place in Kangra was understandable. Emerging from the Gaj Khad, this tributary of the Beas remains quite unknown even in present-day India.

However, the interest in transplanting trout in this remote valley shows that the success of the experiment first in Kashmir and then in Kullu was encouraging for British officers and settlers. They wanted to recreate this experiment in every hill stream in north India. Soon, the request for transplanting trout, supplying eyed ova, sending yearling and fry started pouring in from all around, from Chamba, from Shimla, from Sirmour, even from Garhwal and Kumaon. In many places, enthusiastic anglers were even ready to fund a full-fledged hatchery.

As far as Kangra was concerned, Howell wanted to study the conditions before making any commitment. After a thorough examination of the different streams of Suket and Mandi, his notes were ready. Thus he wrote:

> I examined the Beas and three of its principal tributaries in these States – the whole Suketi basin, the lower waters of the Uhl and the Uttarsal Khad in September, 1913. Of the latter the Uhl contains practically no marketable fish with the exception of the mountain barbel (sal). Both the Uhl and the Uttarsal might well be stocked with brown trout from Kulu. The Uttarsal, like most of the waters in both States, is regularly poisoned from the end

> of April to the break of the rains in July. The poison used is cactus juice. They are called dudhla or balodar (onkar in Kangra), gandri (ganiri in Kangra) and sama. Casting nets are used all the year round with a mesh of 8" bar measure; they kill fish of four inches long and over. The scoop net (jaltri) described below is also used. In September six clips are erected regularly. If mountain barbel were less prolific (a 2 lb. female 15 inches long was found to contain 15,000 ova and the species breeds we know from April to December) there would not be a fish in the Uttarsal. The Uhl is hardly fished at all.

After this study, Howell did not waste any time and sent 250 fry the very next hatching season. Capt. A.T. Banon, a planter, hotelier and early settler of Manali, was given the responsibility of carrying the fry. Banon crossed the Sari pass and successfully planted them in the Uhl.

In fact, much before the Uhl was stocked, trout had reached Kangra. Records show that a Mr Ross, an ICS officer, took the initiative in 1911 and brought 30,000 ova to hatch out in three small streams, Baner, Awa and Bhinnu.

Howell too was taking great interest in propagating trout in the Himalayan streams adjoining Kullu. Cecil Lang details some of these efforts in his book. Thus, of the experiment in Chamba, he writes:

> The Chamba brook trout in the hatchery came to an untimely end in July 1914. This is a pity as the Raja had

taken the greatest interest in them, their growth was extraordinary, and [a] post-mortem showed that they would have spawned last autumn. The Sarain Gharat Hatchery lies rather far down stream, but the water never rose much above 54 degrees which is well below danger point. Apparently during heavy rains surface water containing .06 of ammonia per 100,000 found its way into the tanks. But I do not think this would have done much harm, had they not been otherwise weakened, though I may be wrong. There were 12 deaths among 175 fish up to July 18th. The keeper then became alarmed, and most unfortunately took all the survivors out and placed them in three bath tubs on July 2nd, while he cleaned the ponds. No trout could stand this treatment in summer, and by the 31st all were dead. The 40,000 fish planted in the streams above Chamba, however, remain and will have spawned in the Ravi last autumn, and I am absolutely confident that His Highness will be catching them fairly freely by this time next year for the water is as good as Kulu waters, and has been nearly 50 per cent more heavily stocked.

Meanwhile, Shimla, the summer capital of British India, had also been experimenting with brown trout. The president of the municipal committee, a man called Kettlewell, took the initiative to stock the streams and ravines of this hill station. In 1910, he stocked the Nauti Khadd, below the Fagu bungalow, with 9,000 ova in Mr Mitchell's 'pahari' boxes, of which 7,000 were reported to be hatched out. He also stocked 3,000 ova in a feeder of the Aswini stream but no development of these ova was reported. The next year he stocked a number of streams on a large scale – 2,000 in Nauti Khadd, 2,000 in Giri above Kot Khai, 1,000 in a tributary of Giri near Junga, 10,000 in the Gaus river, 5,000 in the Sakli river, 10,000 in the Nogh river and 5,000 in the Machhada river. It was later reported that the experiment was very successful in the latter four streams and a large number of fry were hatched out.

The problem with the Shimla region was that there were a number of small streams but no major river in the vicinity. So it could never be a major angling destination. The focus soon shifted to other hill stations. Stocking the hill streams with brown trout had now become easier since there were two options to source ova from, Kashmir and Kullu. Places in Kumaon and Kangra tried their luck from both. Within a few years, when things settled, a clear demarcation of geographical areas emerged for both Kashmir and Kullu. While Kullu was supplying ova for the hills of modern-day Himachal Pradesh and Uttarakhand, hatcheries in Kashmir were stocking the streams of Ladakh, Gilgit, Baltistan, Skardu and the Neelam Valley (some of the latter in modern-day Pakistan).

Gilgit, an important stop on the ancient silk route, presented the biggest challenge for the completion of Mitchell's idea. Though it was just 200 miles from Srinagar, getting there involved crossing several high-altitude passes. Lt. Col. A.B. Dew, assistant political agent of the British empire, and another officer, Lt. Col. Macpherson, were determined to plant trout in this cold desert climate. Mitchell remarked that they bore all the expense of the attempt. A trained man from Harwan established a hatchery there. A first effort failed, but a second succeeded. Although the trout could be established in only one stream of this area, it was enough for the officers of the agency to enjoy a fair amount of trout fishing.

The local Rajas had also started to take an interest in brown trout. They were good shikaris but angling had not previously been a favoured recreation. There were two reasons behind their growing interest in trout. First, that it was being projected as a future source of revenue, in terms of fishing licences and for large scale fish trade. Second, it gave them an opportunity to ingratiate themselves with imperial officials, who were of course very fond of trout angling.

Consider, thus, the interest taken by Keerti Sah, Maharaja of Tehri state, in stocking the different streams of the Garhwal region. In 1910, he established two hatcheries: one at Kaldyani (in the Uttarkashi district of what is now Uttarakhand state) on the bank of the beautiful cold stream of the Asi Ganga; and the other at Talwari (in modern Chamoli district) on the bank of the Pindar river, which originates from the Pindari glacier. Within a year, small yearlings were transplanted in rivers and lakes like Dodi Tal, Balkhila Gad, Rupin-Supin, Madhu Ganga, etc., apart from the Asiganga and Pindar. Since the temperature and other natural conditions were suitable for this exotic fish, brown trout established itself successfully in Garhwal.

While the streams of Garhwal were being stocked, the neighbouring Kumaon region was not far behind. In 1910, a trout hatchery was established at Bhowali, 8 miles from Naini Tal, a beautiful lake in the lower Kumaon hills. The eponymous town around the lake was the summer capital of the United Provinces at the time and is still a popular hill station. The nearby town of Bhowali had 30,000 eyed ova of brown trout in the first month of that year. After successful hatching, 8,000 fry were put in the Naini Tal while some others were sent to Sat Tal, a group of seven interconnected lakes, also in the area. Another batch of 2,000 fry was kept in the hatchery for breeding purposes. But 1910 was a bad year as, in early October, 25 inches of rain fell non-stop over two days, washing out everything in Bhowali. But the trout that had been put into the Naini Tal were not affected and continued to flourish.

Two years later, in 1912, another batch of 30,000 ova was received at the Bhowali hatchery. This time 9,000 fry were put into the Naini lake, and some others in Naukuchia Tal, a huge nine-cornered lake of the region. Some streams of the area were also stocked. Meanwhile good news came out of Naini Tal: the trout placed there had grown into 1 lb yearlings.

Cecil Lang gives us further details of this particular experiment by quoting the notes of an angler named E.A. Smythies of the Imperial Forest Service. Smythies recorded:

In 1913, there were 60 three-year-old fish in the hatchery and 500 yearlings. The three-year-old fish produced good fertile Ova, which was successfully hatched out. This was very interesting in solving the question whether trout would breed in Kumaon. Unfortunately, while the fry were still in the hatching boxes, one night the pipe supplying water became blocked up with leaves, and in the morning all the little fry were found dead. In 1914, we obtained 12,000 Ova from the stock fish, from which 3,500 healthy fry were successfully reared, and partly distributed amongst the surrounding lakes and streams. A considerable number of the older fish were attacked by a growth in the gills (Carcinoma of the Thyroid Gland) and died. Specimens of diseased fish were sent to Mr. Southwell, Director of Fisheries, Bengal. In 1915, the attack of carcinoma continued very severely and did considerable harm, Mr. Southwell's report was received during the year, and he described the disease, and suggested remedial measures to check it. Very fortunately his invaluable suggestions proved most successful, and by the end of the year, the disease was practically stamped out. It had, however, made great inroads into the stock of breeding fish, and threw back the development of the hatchery. However, 15,000 Ova were obtained, from which 7,000 fry were hatched out. Of these 600 were kept for stock, and the rest put out in lakes and streams.

Within a few years, there were attempts to stock almost every lake of the region, but apart from those in the immediate vicinity of Naini Tal, the water at other lakes in lower Kumaon, like Bhim Tal, Sat Tal, Naukuchia Tal and Malwa Tal, was too warm for brown trout.

At some distance from these lakes was the newly formed Gohna Lake, locally known as Durmi Tal. It was located in Garhwal and was the biggest lake in the entire region. This lake was formed as the result of a big landslide in September 1893, which occurred near a village named Gohna. Some 5,000 million tonnes of rock mass had fallen from a 900-metre-high valley flank and blocked the path of a river called Birhi Ganga, a tributary of the Alaknanda. This resulted in the creation of a 270-metre-high dam. On 22 August 1894, this dam burst and the waters it released flooded the Garhwal region. What remained after this disaster was a huge lake called Gohna.

In 1917, the commissioner of Kumaon, Percy Wyndham (who was also a hunting companion of the great Jim Corbett) decided to establish trout in Gohna. With the help of a local forest officer named A.E. Osmaston, Wyndham stocked the lake and its upper waters with 24,000 ova from the Bhowali hatchery, of which 13,000 hatched out. Later, they stocked the trout in some nearby streams too. Since the conditions of the lake were favourable, trout numbers began to swell naturally. Though remote and obscured behind high hills, the place soon became popular for anglers in search of brown trout.

Stories such as these abound. Every hill stream and lake in the Himalaya was at some stage stocked with brown trout. Hatcheries were being built and ova were being transported. Trout angling had become a craze. Almost every British officer was trying his luck with the rod. The sport had also begun to attract travellers. Thus, in the Hindi travel diary of Lt. Col. Sajjan Singh, diwan of Orchha state, we find that, while on the way to Ladakh from Srinagar, he found Europeans camping on the banks of streams at a number of places, all come to fish for trout. (Sajjan Singh himself was in search of ibex to hunt.)

Trout fishing had become a craze as well as a status symbol. Consider thus a letter written in May 1922 to the prime minister of Patiala state by Lt. Col. A.B. Minchin of the Indian Army, who was at the time on the staff of the governor-general of Punjab. The letter ran:

> To,
>
> Sir Daya Kishan (Diwan Bahadur), K.B.E., C.I.E.
>
> Prime Minister, Patiala State
>
> I informed her excellency of his highness' readiness to help to keep her fish pond supplied with trout, and she asked me to convey her grateful thanks.
>
> What the private secretary to the viceroy suggests is that about 30 live trout weighing from half a pound to about two pounds each should be sent to him to be put in the pond which will be ready in a week hence, and then if there is any state official in Simla to whom intimation could be given when more trout are needed, Sir G. De Montmorency would give timely notice. The trout will be used only for Lady Reading.

Kindly let me know whether the above arrangements are feasible.

A. B. Minchin

Unfortunately, available records do not tell us whether these 30 live trout were arranged to grace the pond of Lady Reading, wife of Lord Reading, viceroy of India.

X

ENVIRONMENTAL IMPACT

THE KEY DRIVER FOR TRANSPLANTING TROUT IN INDIA, AS elsewhere in the world, was its recreational possibilities for British colonialists. The fish was shipped across the seven seas just for the pleasure of the hunt. And for this it was given a privileged pass into the most beautiful rivers, streams and lakes of the Himalaya and peninsular India – with public money and without any thought to local flora and fauna. There was no concern for native species that were forced to share natural resources with this invasive alien. Moreover, the introduction of trout was not a one-time operation; repeated and extensive stocking programmes had been established to ensure good catches for European anglers.

It is true that ecological and environmental concerns were not given much consideration in those days. The term 'invasive species' was coined much later. The common thinking at the time was that the British were to be credited for an act of benefaction, by introducing a 'superior fish' and adding a new element to the ecological system. And yet there are no records of European streams being enhanced by Indian fish like mahseer or snow trout!

A South African anthropologist, Knut G. Nustad, made some interesting observations in his paper titled 'Wilderness through Domestication: Trout, Colonialism, and Capitalism in South Africa', published in 2018, which are relevant to trout transplantation in India as well. Nustad writes:

> Trout were introduced by the British with the aim of making South African river landscapes more like those of the English countryside at home. In this sense, then, the introduction of trout was, together with the introduction of other species, part of an attempt by the colonists to domesticate the landscape. ...Trout were introduced both to reshape environments to resemble 'home' and, at the same time, to create a specific form of nature, if not wilderness, separate from human society. South African trout, then, are a product of colonial expansion. ...As has been well documented, European colonial expansion involved not just the movement of people, but of animals and plants as well. The landscapes of the colonies were often seen as lacking in plants and animals when compared to nature back home.

In India, like South Africa, Australia and New Zealand, a preparatory study was done each time a stream was stocked. This started with Francis Day, when he was given the responsibility of stocking the streams of the Nilgiris. Frank Mitchell also studied the streams of Kashmir before stocking them with brown trout. H.C. Wilson was the first professional to study the streams of the Nilgiris for rainbow trout stocking. And there is a lot of material by way of proof of the detailed study done by G.C.L. Howell in the Kullu valley.

However, the purpose of all these studies was to ascertain the suitability of streams for trout, and never the obverse – the impact of trout on native fauna. The latter was not studied in detail, neither before nor after stocking operations. Information on the impact of trout on aquatic fauna in India is lacking even today.

G.C.L. Howell seems to have been aware of this aspect. When transplanting trout in the Beas, he wrote in the *Journal of the Bombay Natural History Society*, published in 1915, that 'two species only are native to the Beas above Sultanpur, "Mountain barbel" (Oreinussinuatus) and a small Siluroid or Catfish (Glyptosternum striation). They are known locally as "Gunguli" and "Mochi" [Cobbler] respectively, and the "cobbler" is not sufficiently common to be important. With the barbel it is otherwise. The barbel seem to spawn nearly continuously from March to October, and though the bigger fish – they run up to 3 lbs, or so in weight – drop downstream to the neighbourhood of Sultanpur in winter, the warmer brooks and runners hold fry all the year round. The fecundity of the barbel is the supremely important fact par excellence in connection with trout in the Beas. In the Nilgheris, for instance, acclimatised trout tend to increase faster than their food supply; in many New Zealand rivers the same trouble occurs: but in the Beas there is no danger of the barbel being eaten down, and they undoubtedly form and will form one of the staple foods of our Salmo fario.'

But when Howell continued, 'even if the barbel disappeared, it is most improbable that the food supply would ever give out,' his greater concern for trout is apparent.

In Kashmir, when Frank Mitchell first went to angle in the Arrah river, he was greatly dissatisfied with the fish available in that ideal trout stream. At that time he thought, 'If they could be replaced by the beauties I had loved at home, here was indeed a true angler's paradise.' ('How Trout Were Introduced Into Kashmir' by Frank Mitchell in *Journal of Bombay Natural History Society*, 1931) Later, when he studied the local streams in Kashmir for trout acclimatization, he had somewhat refined his attitude to the native mountain barbel. He was quoted in the *Journal of the Asiatic Society*, in 1939, as saying,

> ...this fish takes its name of (oreinus) "Sinuatus" from its habit of twisting under water when sucking alga and moss off the stones with its thick sucking lips. Thousands of Khont when in their best condition in late autumn used to enter the big springs of the Arrah and Achabal Rivers and remain during winter in the underground streams – the source of these springs. They are, as far as I have seen, really useful in trout water, and it was much against my wish that efforts were made to exterminate

> them in such streams. A gentleman from New Zealand visited Kashmir in the early days and seeing the Oreinus lying in black masses at the bottom of some of the pools in the Arrah River, expressed disbelief in the success of trout there with such quantities of native fish. I laughed at him and told him I knew the relative powers of both fish and that I had no doubt on the subject. I have reason to think, however, that his expressed opinion added much to the disbelief in trout prospects which then existed in the country and did harm later in causing destruction of Oreinus I would have saved. ...In some of my later reports I expressed myself strongly on the subject as the disappearance of Sinuatus synchronized with a great increase of alga and other deleterious matter as well as with a distinct decrease in the average size of trout.

Taking a cue from this, when the eminent Indian pisciculturist S.L. Hora found a decrease in local fish fauna, he directed his colleague Ghulam Mustafa Malik to further study the impact in detail. Malik researched the matter thoroughly and concluded that: 'Brown Trout, a carnivorous fish, flourishes well in association with Oreinua, as the latter keeps the streams clean of the vegetable growth and other deleterious matter and thereby encourages the growth of insect larvae that inhabit rooks and stones and form the food of Brown Trout. Further, its fry provides food for the trout during the season when insects, which form its normal diet, are scarce.' Malik went on to say that it was important to study the native flora and fauna of a stream before introducing foreign species to it, arguing that to not do so would be to threaten the "balance" of nature established after centuries of existence'.

By the time Malik discussed his findings at the Zoology Section of the 26th session of the Indian Science Congress held at Lahore in January 1939, awareness of the impact of acclimatizing alien species had begun to appear across the world. *The Statesman* of Calcutta published three reports on Punjab fisheries in October–November 1934, which started a debate over whether the head of the fisheries department should have been a pisciculturist or an ICS officer. The Bangalore journal *Current Science* strongly favoured the appointment of a pisciculturist to this post, arguing that 'usually there are numerous species of fish of varying sizes in almost every stream and introduction of an exotic species is bound to upset the ecological balance of nature. It is therefore highly desirable to investigate the local fauna and its reaction to the introduced species before undertaking an experiment on large scale.' *Current Science* believed a local expert was necessary to advise the government 'on scientific and administrative problems'.

The debate didn't end there. An anonymous reader shot back a response: 'Alluding to the introduction of trout in hill streams the writer tells us that it is dangerous to try experiments in introducing exotic species. ...He, however, omits to mention that the experiment was undertaken in waters in which only one indigenous species exists, and that too of small economic value.'

'Economic value' was one of the prime drivers of the introduction of a number of fish species to Indian streams without any consideration for their ecological impact. The impact of species like silver carp and tilapia was devastating for many indigenous species and the aquatic ecosystem in general. Silver carp was in fact imported only for commercial farming in controlled conditions, but the fish somehow found its way into natural water bodies.

Trout, on the other hand, was imported to directly stock the mainstream aquatic ecosystem of India. Fortunately, its impact on local fauna was far from devastating. One reason perhaps was that, in the Himalayan region, trout waged a constant battle to survive – despite the temperature and atmospheric conditions being favourable, the availability of adequate food, and enough gravel, rubble and boulders in these streams to make perfect trout water.

In his book *Fish and Fishing in Kulu*, Lt. Col. Richard Humphrey Tyacke spoke about the sudden and brutal floods that the Beas was prone to. As he put it: 'When they come, they are terrifying, whole trees are brought down, bridges washed away, and the water that comes down is almost solid with the result many fishes get choked; and after a heavy flood trout have been found dead on the riverbank, which on examination were found to have their gills filled with black silt which has caused their death.'

This observation ran contrary to the traditional belief that trout not only survive but enjoy floods. But Tyacke faulted the Beas itself. 'In Kulu,' he wrote, 'they are not ordinary floods that the fish have to contend with, but floods caused by deluges of water from mountains up to 15,000 feet, which are precipitated into the river that already has a fall of scores of feet to the mile, deluges that frequently bring down the deposit of many landslips, so that the river is half water and half silt; and under such conditions who can wonder that many fish are choked.'

Brown trout established itself very well in the Asiganga river of the Garhwal Himalaya, and survived there for more than a century. The river originates from a lake called Dodital, which is at an altitude of 3,075 metres. Trout was introduced in both Dodital and the Asiganga in 1910, neither site prone to much human interference. Dodital and some parts of the Asiganga had a native fish, the snow trout, belonging to the sub-family *Schizothoracinae* and locally known as dodi. It was reported that the brown trout of Asiganga was devouring dodi fingerlings, and the extinction of the dodi was predicted.

On the evening of 3 August 2012, a massive cloudburst over the high mountains caused a flash flood in the Asiganga. According to one study, this flood drastically increased the flow of discharged water from 135 to 2,665 cubic metres per second. As many as 35 people died. The flood also caused a significant change in the habitat of the Asiganga. Between June 2017 and June 2018, the National Mission for Sustaining the Himalayan Ecosystem studied the habitat by netting downstream at 14 different points. The study found that brown trout had been extinguished from the river system of the Asiganga, and that dodi fingerlings were present at almost all points. The brown trout had not been able to cope with the brute force of the flash flood, but the snow trout did. As the study concluded: 'Continuous modifications in hydrological patterns over the years must have made the native snow trout much more resilient to natural stochasticity than the exotics; thus helping in their retention.'

Of this episode, *Current Science* remarked:

> Extirpation of the brown trout population in Asiganga is a perfect instance of 'priority effects' in a natural system. Although this invasive species is highly resilient to varied habitats worldwide, the extreme entropy of nature, like the Asiganga flash flood, is a positive indication where nature takes decisions in favour of native biota. Asiganga nevertheless being an unaltered river, would provide equal opportunities to leading freshwater invaders like the brown trout, if environment and habitat favour it in the future. The resurgence of brown trout in Asiganga, if it occurs, would lead to a better understanding of adaptive capabilities of both the brown trout and snow trout; the former towards environmental resistance and the latter towards biological resistance due to the invasive brown trout.

The previous chapter discussed the large Gohna Lake, which emerged on the map suddenly on 25 August 1894 as a result of a geo-climatic change. In 1917, it was stocked with brown trout and soon became one of the finest angling destinations in the Himalaya. The lake continued to attract anglers for the next five decades. But on 20 July 1970, the flooding of the Alaknanda river drained every drop of water from this huge lake. The history of trout in this beautiful lake ended with the flood.

Meanwhile, in peninsular India the biotic impoverishment of the streams and consequent deterioration in the size of Nilgiri trout began to be felt seriously as early as 1913. This resulted in the imposition of angling restrictions on the size and number of trout. Paucity of food was reckoned to be the main reason for this deterioration And many steps were taken to improve the natural food supply and to augment the biota of streams. Coral rocks were placed at the stream head to augment the calcium content of the water. Farms for insects, shrimps, crabs and prawns were constructed to source plenty of food to the royal guest of the streams. Even water weeds were planted to provide shade and shelters to these creatures. To provide better resting places for trout in the summer, boulders were placed and wattle dams were constructed in selected sections. Afforestation of stream banks was taken up. These vigorous efforts were to no avail; neither the size nor the weight of Nilgiri trout increased.

Later, after some further studies on the taxonomy of Nilgiri trout, it was concluded that the trout stock came from several imported species like rainbow trout, *Salmo gairdnerishasta*, Loch Leven, brown trout, *Salmo trutta fario* and the heavily spotted variety of rainbow trout. Some strains of trout called steelhead were also indicated. Another study claimed that whereas pure rainbow trout have 160 scales along the lateral line, trout introduced in Rajamallay showed a scale count of less than 140, which seemed to offer further confirmation that what was known as Nilgiri trout was actually a variety of steelhead.

In sum: the exotic species of fish introduced in peninsular India were far from being in harmony with local ecoclimatic conditions.

XI

TROUT IN INDEPENDENT INDIA

DECEMBER IS THE MONTH THE HIGH HILLS AROUND Mandi, a former princely state now part of Himachal Pradesh, start to receive snowfall. On a cold morning in December 1945, the chief minister of Mandi wrote a letter to the Punjab Government, headquartered in Lahore. The subject of the letter was 'Supply of Trout Ova for Mandi State', and it read: 'The Mandi State Fisheries Departments require 10,000 eyed ova of Brown Trout for Barot Trout Hatchery. The warden of Fisheries Punjab has suggested that the ova can be had from the Kashmir Darbar.'

A month later, on 9 January 1946, the request was forwarded to the external assistant to the resident of Kashmir. The officials of Kashmir took their time to reply. Six weeks later, the Punjab Government got this response: 'The Kashmir government can supply, on payment, 10,000 eyed ova of Brown Trout in the next autumn. They state that delivery has to be taken in Kashmir and that Mandi State shall have to make its own arrangement for transport.'

The letter was forwarded to Mandi State reasonably quickly, within ten days. More than one-and-a-half months later, the chief minister of Mandi enquired about two things: the rate of the eyed ova of brown trout, and cost of the ova packing box. The letter was forwarded to Srinagar from Lahore on 6 August 1946. When no reply arrived for two months, a reminder was sent. A month passed, and another reminder followed. Finally the reply: 'Trout ova can be supplied from the hatchery at Achhabal at the rate of Rs 60/- per thousand of ova. The cost of the packing boxes is approximately estimated not to exceed Rs 40/- in all.'

While this somewhat leisurely and highly specialized official correspondence was going on, India was passing through a crucial period in its modern history. 1946 was the year when it had become quite clear that the transfer of power from colonial rulers to Indian hands was imminent. It was the year when the British Cabinet Mission came to India to finalise the formalities of granting independence. And it was the year when a Constituent Assembly was formed to draft the Constitution of independent India.

1946 gave way to 1947. After the new year dawned, Mandi's chief minister wrote: 'In view of the fact that the Punjab Government have promised to supply trout ova, the Mandi Darbar would not require the supply of ova, so kindly promised by Kashmir Government. Kashmir Government may kindly be informed, accordingly.'

This sudden change in mood reflected the changing political situation. Mandi did not want to invest in a project dear to the outgoing rulers of the country. Rajas and maharajas need no longer curry favour with officials of the Raj.

After India become independent in August 1947, trout fishing started to lose its privileged status in the subcontinent. Soon, trout started to disappear from Indian streams, along with their erstwhile promoters. However, the exit of the British Raj was not the only reason for the disappearance of trout. The sport of angling was not domesticated in India as easily as other imported activities such as cricket, hockey, football or badminton. It did not garner popularity among the middle classes, nor a permanent position as a recreational activity among the upper classes. There was no such thing as an *Indian* community of trout lovers.

That said, angling in India did not owe entirely to its colonial rulers. The text of the chapter 'Matsyavinoda' from the *Manasollasa* (also known as *Abhilashitartha Chintamani*) written by the Kalyani Chalukya king Somesvara in 1127 CE, is regarded by some as the first treatise on the art of angling in India. However, this particular form of the hunt never gained popularity among the royal shikaris, who were passionate about hunting for big game in dense forests. The reasons for this are unclear but the practice of commercial fishing by designated lower castes in precolonial India may have discouraged the elites.

Trout fishing did not flourish after August 1947 either, because the new nation had a new set of priorities. What independent India needed most was food security for its large population and rapid industrial development to compete with the rest of the world. For food security, it needed rapid growth in production and productivity in the agriculture sector, which could not be achieved without dealing effectively with the vagaries of a monsoon climate. For industrial growth, on the other hand, along with the fast-expanding urban footprint of the population, the country needed to generate a large amount of electricity to meet the increasing demand.

Jawaharlal Nehru, the first prime minister of independent India, was determined to achieve both goals. A series of 'five-year plans' resulted in the large-scale construction of dams to provide water for both irrigation and power-generation. In 1963, at the dedication of the Bhakra Dam, the most ambitious of all such projects, Nehru famously called these mammoth dams the 'temples of New India'.

Building large dams became a national obsession. The taming of every possible stream was on the drawing board. Within a few decades, India became one of the world's most prolific dam-builders, with more than 4,300 large dams built and many more in the pipeline. Virtually any road in the Himalaya, the Western Ghats or the Nilgiris leads to a dam after a few miles.

Dams are a barrier built across a stream or river to confine and check the flow of water for human consumption. At the same time, they also transform the ecosystem of the water body. These dams in India are estimated to have submerged about 37,500 sq km – a massive area almost the size of Switzerland – that has resulted in large-scale destruction of biodiversity. The impact on aquatic biodiversity of hill streams in particular has been profound and often irreversible.

Fish populations in general, and trout in particular, are highly dependent upon the characteristics of their aquatic habitat for their biological functions. Trout is a migratory fish. It requires different environments for the main phases of its life cycle – reproduction, production of juveniles, growth and sexual maturation. Trout is an anadromous fish; it migrates upriver in search of a safe place to spawn. There it forms a depression in gravel, where female trout lay eggs and the male releases milt over it. When the construction of dams began to block this natural process of migration, trout started to disappear.

Even before a dam is completed, its construction obstructs the stream, reducing the water in channels with excessive silt and depleting the oxygen in the water. All this makes it difficult for fish to survive in a habitat where they once flourished. As the official website of the Nilgiris states, 'After the commissioning of hydroelectric power projects in this district, the course of water streams has changed drastically, negatively affecting the trout fishery. At present, trout fishery has lost its original significance and needs a systematic revamp for sustainable development.'

However, the construction of dams large and small is not the only reason for the rapid depletion of trout. Take the Beas River in Kullu, once considered the finest trout water in India. A full 18 km stretch of the river, from Manali to Katrain, is still pristine trout water, with no dam or power project in the area or even upstream. And yet trout can hardly be found there now.

The environmentalist and Kullu resident S.B. Raizada has studied this decline in some detail. He believes that the ecosystem of the Beas, which supported every stage of the lifecycle of trout, has been grievously disturbed. Large-scale commercial exploitation of the forest, particularly of the citrulline-rich alder wood for apple crates, as well as the destruction of other soil-conserving and cooling varieties of plants and trees, has disturbed the biocycle of the water body, resulting in the depletion of its fish. River beds were uprooted by resultant floods and increased silt load. In his paper, 'Remaking of the Himalayan Trout Waters', published in *Cheetal* in 1986, a journal of the Wildlife Preservation Society of India, Raizada offered several reasons for the disappearance of trout. He listed the reduction of natural breeding opportunities (in some cases to 10 per cent of the original available space); low food input; physical interference from humans owing to the proximity of habitations; pollution from human sources; and increased pressure from angling.

Raizada studied the Beas and its tributaries in Kullu in the period 1963–83. He found that there was 40 per cent less food available for the fish with a commensurate reduction of green cover on the river banks and catchment area. He wrote: 'This cover has come down dangerously from 76% in the 19th century to less than 22%. ...Rivers have much less tree cover and the bushes are cleared away, replaced by regular dwelling or fields causing a physical disturbance to trout and adding greatly to the rate of pollution. The same has been the fate of natural nurseries. ...The river bank cover has shrunk down to 20% in 1985 from the level of 1962, that in turn reduced the number of pools also to 20% and simultaneously raising the "rapids" area.' The process of degradation has not been reversed in subsequent decades, despite grandiose claims about afforestation and conservation.

What is true about the Beas in Kullu is also true about most other rivers and streams of India. Nonetheless, there are a few streams in the country where one can catch trout in any angling season. In Himachal Pradesh, these streams include the Tirthan, Sainj, Parbati, Uhl and Lambadug. The Tirthan is the most popular. Part of the Banjar region of Kullu district, and somewhat removed from the main tourist circuit, its environs are relatively untouched compared to other rivers in the area. Moreover, there exist no hindrances for the complete biological functioning of the trout since the Himachal Government decided not to build dams or power plants on this river. From Nagni to Largi, a 20-km-long stretch of this river is earmarked as trout water, with a hatchery in Nagni to restock it regularly. The same hatchery also stocks the nearby Sainj and Parbati rivers. A hatchery at Barot, a beautiful and scenic valley of Mandi district, where the Lambadug joins the Uhl, supplies these last two rivers. However, the stretch of trout water here is limited and must remain so, since there is a dam and a power plant downstream.

Every year, during the angling season, anglers flock to Tirthan and licences are issued. They usually return with a good catch, though they are not always satisfied. It is said that the availability and size of brown trout have been decreasing every year. This may be the case with regard toother streams too. During the 2013 angling season, the Trout Conservation and Angling Association of Kullu organised a competition on the banks of the Parbati, near Kasol town, where 20 anglers struggled to catch fish. The anglers caught 18 rainbow trout during the competition. The biggest catch weighed about 850 grams. The chief guest Jimmy Johnson remarked, 'There was a time when they used to catch 3 kg trout in the river.'

It is the same state of affairs in the hills of the Western Ghats. Thus K.L. Sehgal, of the Directorate of Coldwater Fisheries Research, collected data from different studies on the size of rainbow trout in peninsular India. He wrote:

> The analysis of creel census data from 1936 to 1952 revealed that the trout in nine streams of the Nilgiris had not shown an appreciable decrease in average size.

> It remained around 180 g in weight on an annual average basis. The catch per rod in relation to fishing pressure [in census data from 1936 to 1952] showed a decline from 12 fish to 3.6 fish between 1936 and 1943. From 1944 until 1952 there were narrow fluctuations in catch per rod. There was, however, a marked decrease in catch per angler between 1936 (12 fish) and 1952 (6.6 fish). ...The true stream fishing for trout is carried out in the Lakidi and Deverbetta streams which empty into Upper Bhavani Reservoir. In 1967–1970 the average size of rainbow ranged between 290–403 g in Lakidi against 321–386 g in Deverbetta. The data revealed that an increase in fishing pressure resulted in a fall of the average size in both streams. The maximum size of a rainbow caught during 1967–68 to 1969–70 was 2.2 kg in Lakidi against 0.4 kg in [the] Deverbetta stream. There is no published account available on the trout catches in the Palni Hills.

Meanwhile, the website of the department of fisheries, Government of Kerala, tells us that 'overfishing, destructive fishing, juvenile fishing, degradation/ loss of habitats, pollution of water bodies, climate change, mangrove deforestation, sand mining, the introduction of exotic fishes, the infestation of aquatic weeds, shrinkage of water resources etc. pose serious threat to fish diversity and abundance in the inland water bodies of the state'.

In the Western Ghats, the temperature of the rivers, streams and lakes was optimum for rainbow trout when it was first introduced. On the other hand, brown trout were never established because the water temperature was too high. A century later, global warming has endangered rainbow trout too. A few sites where they are still to be found are the Rajamallay and Eravikulam streams, which are stocked from a hatchery established in 1943 on the Kanan Devan Company's Nyamakad estate. This hatchery is located at an altitude of 6,500 ft and is adjacent to the Eravikulam National Park, a Project Tiger sanctuary and home to the endangered Nilgiri tahr. It is probably the only privately owned project for natural trout varieties.

Kashmir, once known as a haven for anglers, is paradise no longer. The state's department of fisheries claims that trout can be caught in a number of streams. They provide a long list: the Lidder, Wangath, Gurez, Hamal, Lam, Sindh, Kishenganga, Sukhnag, Doodhganga, Erin, Ferozpur (Tangmarg), Bringi, Aharbal, Hirpora, Dachigam, Kokernag, Naristan, Madhumati and Nowbugh. The department runs more than two dozen trout hatcheries and breeding centres, but this infrastructure is unable to attract anglers in numbers. The state has been beset by continuous political disturbance and militancy for several decades now. Before this, the state's devoted visitors included a sizeable number of anglers, who came mainly from overseas.

Terrorism drove the visitors away from Kashmir but not pollution. Everywhere in Kashmir, trout is declining due to a deadly blend of pollution, human intervention and climate change. Farooz Ahmad Bhat, senior assistant professor at the Sher-i-Kashmir Institute of Agriculture Sciences, has studied the decline of trout population. He finds that, 'In most of the water bodies of Kashmir valley the fish catch per unit effort has decreased over the years. ...The ecological degradation in their habitats mostly due to the lifting of sand, boulders, pebbles and stones from the river beds illegally has affected their population over the years.' He also points to the use of biocides, heavy deforestation around streams and the construction of power plants.

Large-scale commercial exploitation of the streams is intensifying the problem. An article from Srinagar, published in the *Indian Express*, on 12 April 2011, reads:

> Endangering almost half of Kashmir's famed trout habitat and in violation of the J&K Fisheries Act, the state government has issued tenders for the extraction of boulders and gravel from as many as 36 freshwater streams. ...The tenders, issued on April 3 by the state's Geology and Mining department, come after no-objection certificates (NOC) were issued to set up two large stone-crushers right on the banks of the most critical freshwater streams: in Lidder Valley in Pahalgam (South Kashmir) and Arin in Bandipore (North Kashmir) ...Directly affected are the 10 biggest trout-populated freshwater streams, including the Brengi stream in Anantnag, the Lidder in Pahalgam, the Arin and Madhumati streams in Bandipore, and the Feroz Pora stream in the Gulmarg-Tangmarg valley. All for a 'royalty' of Rs 3 crore.

Meanwhile, the demand pattern for fish in India is also changing. The demand for game fish is diminishing and that for table fish increasing. The fisheries departments of Himalayan states have changed their priorities in response. Commercial farming of trout is a new trend, expanding across the hills, with farmers coming forward in large numbers. The business of trout farming is growing to meet the increasing demand for exotic table fish in urban India.

In Jammu and Kashmir alone, there are more than 533 such ventures in the private sector. In the financial year 2019–20, the state produced more than 600 tonnes of rainbow trout. Himachal Pradesh generated 685 tonnes in this period. Trout is providing employment, not only in the farming sector but for hatcheries, rearing units, trout feed mills, and the packaging and logistics sectors. This business is growing at a speed that matches the growth of the poultry business in other parts of India.

Even as the business of farmed trout is in the ascendant, organic trout is increasingly disappearing from its habitat. They are vanishing entirely from some regions, but so are other fish. Of India's more than 2,500 species of fish, virtually all now face some level of threat.

The most chilling example of the ruination of habitat concerns the tiger of India's rivers, the mighty mahseer. Like trout, mahseer is also a coldwater migratory fish. Although it is found at a slightly lower altitude, there are some places where mahseer and trout share the same habitat. In most places, the condition of mahseer is even worse than that of trout. According to the World Wide Fund for Nature, mahseer 'have suffered severe population declines in much of its distribution range, and are now considered threatened due to pollution, habitat loss and over-fishing. There is a dearth of information on habitat, feeding and breeding ecology of the species. Mahseer is a sensitive species that can barely tolerate a modified water environment. This is evident from the decrease in its size (length) recorded over the last century, size composition (predominance of young/immature individuals) and reduced share in the catch (as low as 5% from 40–50%) from its distribution ranges.' *Hornbill* from January 2014, a magazine published by the Bombay Natural History Society, further tells us, 'Though mahseer contributes in a major way to inland fisheries, they are the most threatened groups in the mega fishes. Unsustainable fishing and dams are some of the major threats to the mahseer.' Mahseer has also featured on the Red List of Threatened Species, prepared regularly by the International Union for Conservation of Nature.

Saving the mahseer in India may be even more important than saving trout. If all the trout from India vanish, there will still be species of trout elsewhere in the world. Not so the mahseer: if it disappears from the Indian subcontinent, it will become extinct. Saving the mahseer in its original aquatic habitat will mean saving the once exotic but now successfully indigenized trout too.

EPILOGUE

WHENEVER I THINK OF TROUT IN INDIAN STREAMS, I think of Jimmy Johnson. The 83-year-old has been witness to much of the trout's history in the country, from a period when trout were abundant to their current highly diminished state.

Jimmy lives on a large estate in Raisen, a small but very beautiful stopover on the scenic route from Kullu to Manali, set on the banks of the Beas. His speech reflects an all-encompassing love for the Kullu valley, but the one word that comes up repeatedly is 'trout'.

Jimmy is a descendant of Europeans who settled in the Kullu Valley in the latter half of the nineteenth century. These were people who embraced the valley for its beauty and peace, and then created a world of their own. They hunted here, planted orchards here and, by writing about it continuously, made it a tourist destination. And of course they brought trout, a fish which gives Kullu a distinct identity on the tourism map even today. For these devoted anglers, trout fishing was a favourite hobby, when not an obsession.

But everything changed within a few decades. Most of these Europeans left their beloved valley even before India became independent. But the Johnsons were one of the two British families who decided to stay on. They had not only adapted to local life and climate but also embraced its cultural and social practices. They even married within the community.

Jimmy's father, Lt. Col. C.R. Johnson, was in the British Indian Army, and made his home here in the valley after retiring. After his first marriage broke up, he married a local woman and Jimmy is their child.

Jimmy spent his childhood on the banks of the Beas, which gave him plenty of opportunity to observe various angling practices. His father was a very good angler who would often go fishing with his rod, reel, hooks, tackles, etc. However, Jimmy learnt angling not from his father but by watching the famous angler of the valley, T. Tyson (the author of *Trout Fishing in Kulu,* 1941). Jimmy's school was in Mahili, across the river from Katrain where Tyson used to fish virtually every day. And Jimmy would watch the great angler while playing with his friends on the left bank of the river. He started to like Tyson's 'game' more than his own childish ones, seeing it as 'an interesting game in which delicious lunch and dinner were also guaranteed'.

Jimmy's new hobby soon consumed him. He started to learn insider tricks while still very young, and caught his first trout before he was in his teens. Later, he began to travel the length and the breadth of the valley to unearth all the possible secrets behind catching trout.

He has caught trout in almost every river, every stream and every nullah of Kullu. In the Beas, Tirthan, Parbati, Kasol Nullah, Solang Nullah, Chakki Nullah, Sarvari... even in the Uhl, far from the Kullu valley. 'However, no river was as plentiful as the Beas,' he says. 'Elsewhere there were small fish. In the Tirthan and other streams, a fish bigger than one-and-a-half to two pounds was not available, whereas fish ranging from seven to ten pounds could easily be caught in the Beas.'

Jimmy still remembers one eventful day when he went fishing in the morning. After a short wait, a trout raised itself from the bottom and became his prey after giving a good fight. It was a magnificent eight-pounder, the biggest trout he had ever caught.

'But now such a big trout cannot even be thought of,' he says. 'Once, the Beas was a river of quick-sighted trout, now you can rarely find them. I used to go angling at least once or twice a week and return with lots of trout in my bucket. I caught that trout in the early fifties, when trout were in abundance. Then they suddenly disappeared.'

A big flood in the late fifties changed everything overnight. Most of the trout were swept away, and angling's glory days never returned. The flood also changed the infrastructure established for trout. Jimmy recalls: 'The small stream that was used for the trout hatchery dried up, and with that any remaining hope of restocking the Beas also dried up. Neither did the trout came back on their own nor did anybody try [to bring them back] with any conviction. A new government was not ready to spend its resources on such a project.'

Even at his advanced age, Jimmy keeps himself updated about new developments. 'Now there are only two trout hatcheries in Himachal,' he says, 'One on the banks of the Uhl at Barot in Mandi district, another at Nagini in the Tirthan valley. There are trout in these rivers but not in the Beas. Some trout are also found in the Parbati river at Kasol, but these are descendants of the trout stocked here long ago. Nobody is stocking it with new trout. So many buildings are constantly being built around Parbati, how can the trout live in such a river? The situation is the same here in Kullu. Lots and lots of buildings being built here, more than in Kasol... The environment has also been changing for the last few years, Global warming is happening. The trout are disappearing. Earlier the water that used to fall from the different streams into the Beas was clean, now it is muddy, with a lot of silt in it. When it rains, it becomes very dirty.'

Jimmy still has his angling licence renewed every year. When the fishing season arrives after the long, hard winter in this high-altitude valley, he leaves the house with all his equipment. His knees not being as strong as they used to be, he can no longer climb too high or descend too low and goes where the river is easily accessible, by the side of the road. He sometimes spends hours on the bank, but rarely catches any fish. Usually the only compensation for his empty creel is the fine scenery all around him. But he is a true angler; every unsuccessful trip whets his appetite to return.

'There is no shortage of trout to eat,' says Jimmy during a phone interviw, of the rainbow trout farms set up all over Kullu. 'People eat it a lot, I also eat it sometimes. But brown trout tastes so good, rainbow trout cannot compete with this taste.'

For most Kullu residents, though, brown trout is virtually history. Jimmy Johnson's forefathers had a dream and they left no stone unturned to make it a reality. A century later, Jimmy is left with nostalgic memories of a trout-abundant childhood. And, of course, his own dreams.

WORKS CITED

CHAPTER I: NO TRUE TROUT IN INDIA

'A Fisherman's Letter to his Chum in India', *Bentley's Miscellany*, Vol 41, 1857.

Edward Balfour, *The Cyclopædia of India and of Eastern and Southern Asia*, London: B. Quaritch, 1885.

Edward Charles Buck, *The Sportsman's Book for India,* ed. F.G. Aflalo, London: Horace Marshall & Son, 1904.

Skene Dhu, *The Angler in India or The Mighty Mahseer*, Madras: Higginbotham & Co., 1906.

Henry S. Polehampton, *A memoir, letters, and diary of the Rev. Henry S. Polehampton, M.A.*, London: R. Bentley, 1858.

J.L. Dickie, *Forty Years of Trout and Salmon Fishing*, London: Health Cranton, 1919.

G.H. Lacy, *North Punjab Fishing Club Anglers' Handbook*, Calcutta: W. Newman & Co., 1888.

John McClelland, 'Mountain trout of Kemaon', *The Journal of the Asiatic Society of Bengal*, Vol. 4, 1835.

Olive Optic, *Across India: Or, Live Boys in the Far East*, Boston: Lee and Shepard, 1895.

Charles Raikes, *The Englishman in India*, London: Longmans Green & Co., 1867.

Mayne Reid, *The Plant Hunters; or, Adventures Among the Himalaya Mountains*, Boston: Ticknor and Fields, 1858.

The Imperial Gazetteer of India, Vol. 1, 1881

Henry Sullivan Thomas, *The Rod in India*, London: Hamilton, Adam & Co., 1873.

S.J. Thomson, *The Silent India: Being Tales and Sketches of the Masses*, Edinburgh and London: William Blackwood and Sons 1913.

W. Walker, *Angling in the Kumaun Lakes*, Calcutta: Thacker, Spink & Co., 1888.

CHAPTER II: SUCCESS IN TASMANIA

Papers & Proceedings of the Royal Society of Van Diemen's Land, Vol II, 1852.

Charles Rangeley-Wilson, *Silt Road: The Story of a Lost River*, London: Chatto & Windus, 2013.

CHAPTER III: IT ALL BEGAN WITH FAILURE

Major Bagnell, *The Sportsman's Book For India*, ed. F.G. Aflalo, London: Horace Marshall & Son, 1904.

F. B. Bevans, *Madras District Gazetteers: Malabar and Anjengo*, Madras: Government Press, 1908.

J.S.C. Eagan, *The Nilgiri Guide And Directory*, Madras: The S.P.C.K. Press, 1916.

W. Francis, *The Nilgiris*, Madras: Government Press, 1908.

Proceedings of the Madras Government, No. 2.262, 5th August 1869.

P.J.P. Whitehead and P.K. Talwar, 'Francis Day (1829-1889) and His Collections of Indian Fishes', *Bulletin of the British Museum (Natural History)*, Vol. 5, No. i, London, 1976.'

CHAPTER IV: TROUT IN THE KASHMIR VALLEY

Col. Unwin, *The Sportsman's Book For India*, ed. F.G. Aflalo, London: Horace Marshall & Son, 1904.

Philip K. Crowe, 'Trout Fishing in Kashmir', *Journal of Bombay Natural History Society*, Volume 53, 1955.

Skene Dhu, *The Angler in India or The Mighty Mahseer*, Madras: Higginbotham & Co., 1906.

Foreign Departments Notes, Internal-B, No. 424, National Archives of India, June 1906.

Walter R. Lawrence, *The Valley of Kashmir*, London: Henry Frowde, 1895.

Frank Mitchell, 'How trout were introduced in Kashmir', *Journal of Bombay Natural History Society*, Vol. 26, 1926.

Lt. Col. Alban Wilson, *Trout fishing in Kashmir*, Calcutta: Thacker Spink, 1920.

CHAPTER V: TROUT IN CEYLON

Philip K. Crowe, *Diversions Of A Diplomat In Ceylon*, Princeton: D Van Nostrand Company, 1956.

Qtd. Skene Dhu, *The Mighty Mahseer and Other Fish; or Hints to Beginners on Indian Fishing*, Madras: Higginbotham & Co. 1923.

E. B. Maeston, *The Fishing Gazette*, July 22, 1905.

Colonel W. Molesworth and J. Bryant, 'Trout Culture in the Nilgiris', Bombay: *Journal of the Bombay Natural History Society*, Vol 27, 1912.

Tropical agriculturist and magazine of the Ceylon Agricultural Society, Peradeniya: Ceylon Agricultural Society, Vol 7, 1887-1888.
Philip K. Crowe, *Diversions Of A Diplomat In Ceylon*, Princeton : D Van Nostrand Company, 1956

CHAPTER VI: TROUT FINALLY COMES TO THE NILGIRIS

Major Bagnell, *The Sportsman's Book For India*, ed. F.G. Aflalo, London: Horace Marshall & Son, 1904.

E.R.C. Davidar, *Whispers from the Wild*, India: Penguin Random House, 2012.

Colonel W. Molesworth and J. Bryant, 'Trout Culture in the Nilgiris', *Journal of the Bombay Natural History Society*, Vol. 27, 1921.

Madras (India: State) Fisheries Bureau, *Madras Fisheries Bulletin*, Vol 12, 1921. Web. Biodiversity Heritage Library. https://www.biodiversitylibrary.org/item/18925#page/5/mode/1up.

Tropical agriculturist and magazine of the Ceylon Agricultural Society, Peradeniya: Ceylon Agricultural Society, Vol 7, 1887-1888. Philip K. Crowe, *Diversions Of A Diplomat In Ceylon*, Princeton : D Van Nostrand Company, 1956

CHAPTER VII: TROUT IN KULLU

Civil and Military Gazette, 22 February, 1910.

Skene Dhu, *The Angler In India or The Mighty Mahseer*, Madras: Higginbotham & Co., 1923.

Qtd. Skene Dhu, *The Mighty Mahseer and Other Fish; or Hints to Beginners on Indian Fishing*, Madras: Higginbotham & Co. 1923.

G.C.L. Howell, 'The Making of a Himalayan Trout Water', *Journal of the Bombay Natural History Society*, Vol. 24, 1915-17.

Lt. Col. Richard Humphrey Tyacke, *Fish and Fishing in Kulu*, Calcutta : Thacker, Spink& Co., 1919.

Mrs. Richard Humphrey Tyacke, *How I Shot My Bears: Or, Two Years' Tent Life in Kullu and Lahoul*, London: S. Low, Marston, 1893.

T. Tyson, *Trout Fishing in Kulu*, Lahore: The Civil and Military Gazette Ltd., Second Edition, 1941.

CHAPTER VIII: TROUT IN TRAVANCORE

Jijo Jayaraj, "Conflict With The Game: 'Shikar' And The 'White' Coloniser", *Misbah*, Vol. 15, 2016.

W.S. Mackay, 'Trout of Travancore', *Journal of the Bombay Natural History Society*, Vol. 45, 1944-45.

Samuel Mateer, *Native life in Travancore*, London: W.H. Allen & Co., 1883.

CHAPTER IX: TROUT, TROUT, EVERYWHERE

Skene Dhu, *The Angler In India or The Mighty Mahseer*, Madras: Higginbotham & Co., 1923.

G.C.L. Howell, *Punjab Civil Secretariat Notes*, Nos. 133/3413, File No. 225, 1913.

CHAPTER X: ENVIRONMENTAL IMPACT

G.C.L. Howell, 'The Making of a Himalayan Trout Water', *Journal of the Bombay Natural History Society*, Vol. 24, 1915-17.

'Inland Fisheries in India', *Current Science*, Vol. 3, 1934-35.

'Letter to editor', *Current Science*, Vol. 4, 1935.

Frank Mitchell, qtd, *Journal of the Royal Asiatic Society of Bengal*, Vol. 5, 1936.

Ghulam Mustafa Malik, *Journal of the Royal Asiatic Society of Bengal*, Vol. 5, 1936.

Knut G. Nustad, 'Wilderness through Domestication. Trout, Colonialism, and Capitalism in South Africa', *Domestication*

Gone Wild, eds. Heather Anne Swanson, Marianne Elisabeth Lien and Gro B. Ween, USA: Duke University Press, 2018.

Lt. Col. Richard Humphrey Tyacke, *Fish and Fishing in Kulu*, Calcutta: Thacker, Spink & Co., 1919.

'When Nature Decides who Stays and who Goes', *Current Science*, Vol. 117, July 2019.

CHAPTER XI: TROUT IN INDEPENDENT INDIA

Farooz Ahmad Bhat, qtd, 'The troubled trout of Kashmir', The Third Pole, April 18, 2016. <https://www.thethirdpole.net/en/climate/the-troubled-trout-of-kashmir/>

'Golden mahseer', World Wildlife Fund, No date. <https://www.wwfindia.org/about_wwf/priority_species/threatened_species/golden_mahseer/>

Hornbill, The Bombay Natural History Society, January 2014.

Muzamil Jaleel, 'J&K govt bends rules to drain half of Valley's trout streams' Indian Express, April 12, 2011. <https://indianexpress.com/article/news-archive/web/jk-govt-bends-rules-to-drain-half-of-valleys-trout-streams/>

S. B. Raizada, 'Remaking of the Himalayan Trout Waters', *Cheetal*, Vol. 27, No. 3, June 1986.

K.L. Sehgal, 'Cold Water Fish and Fisheries in the Western Ghats, India', *Fish and Fisheries at Higher Altitudes: Asia*, Rome: Food and Agriculture Organization of the United Nations, 1999.